*When We Share
the Bible with Children*

When We Share the Bible with Children

by
Elizabeth B. Jones

Beacon Hill Press of Kansas City
Kansas City, Missouri

Revised Edition, 1977

Copyright 1962, by Beacon Hill Press

ISBN: 0-8341-0488-1

Printed in the United States of America

Photo credits:

Roy Lynn, 8, 41, 114, 119
Florence Sharp, 32
Tom Stack, 36
Latham, 58
Hedgecoth, 72
Clark and Clark, 80
Saner, 86
Cliburn, 102, 106

Contents

1. To All Generations — 9
2. Rightly Dividing the Word of Truth — 31
3. The Bible and the Nursery Child — 59
4. The Bible and the Kindergarten Child — 71
5. Primaries and the Bible — 85
6. Older Elementary Children and the Bible — 103

Instructions for Receiving Christian Service Training Credit

1. This is the text for the First Series Unit 216a, "Children and the Bible." Six 50-minute sessions, or the equivalent in time, are required.
2. Your class should be registered with the general office at least three weeks before your first class session. This will allow time for the office to get the class report forms and individual registration slips to you. Also, it will help get texts on time.
3. Each pupil must be present for five of the six sessions to receive credit. Exceptions to this may be given only by permission from the general office.
4. Examinations are optional with the teacher.
5. Please send in the class report to the General Christian Service Training Office upon completion of the course.

For further information consult your local Christian Service Training director or write . . .

CHRISTIAN SERVICE TRAINING
6401 The Paseo
Kansas City, Missouri 64131

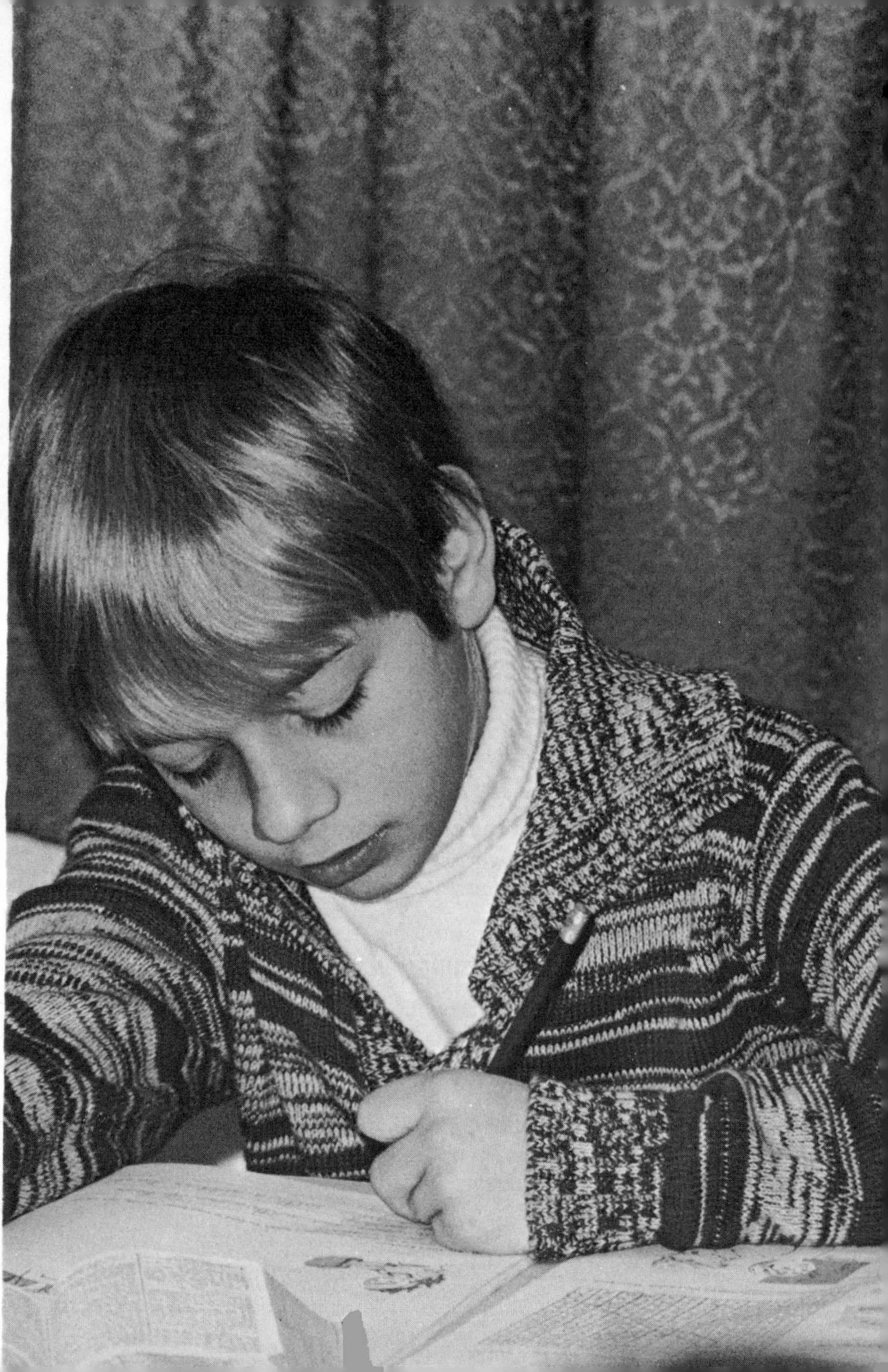

1/

*For the Lord is good; his mercy is everlasting;
and his truth endureth to all generations*
(Psalm 100:5).

To All Generations

PART ONE:

The Book We Share

The Bible is a wonderful Book. Within its pages are found the world's finest poetry, drama, and narration. It is not primarily a book of history, yet it records historical events of greatest importance. It is not intended as a book of science, yet its scientific accuracy is proved again and again. Thoughtful people of this day are asking, "What does the Bible have to say?" Archaeologists are using the Bible as a guide to the discovery of ancient ruins. The information the Bible contains has been most helpful in the rebuilding of the new nation of Israel.

The prophecies of the Bible have been and are being fulfilled with amazing accuracy. The dark picture on the world's horizon today appears much like a jig-saw puzzle to us. We cannot in our own limited vision see how all the pieces fit together to bring about the final outcome. A careful reading of the Bible, however, tells us that God, the Author of the Book, knows the complete picture and is working out His ultimate plan with wisdom and justice.

Yet all these important and interesting facts about the Bible are not the chief reasons why we study it carefully.

Why then do we study? Why are we so deeply concerned with sharing the Bible with our children? The answer is simply this: We believe the Bible to be more than just a great book. We believe it to be the inspired Word of God given to us to reveal God's plan of salvation. It is the Book through which comes the clear shining of the message of God. It tells us of God's being and character, His redeeming love, His ways of working, and His gift of eternal life through our Lord Jesus Christ.

The Bible Speaks to Our Hearts

A young Kekchi Indian sits by the side of an American missionary in the wilds of Guatemala. Spread out on the desk before them are writing materials and many different translations of the Bible. With the help of the young Indian, the missionary is laboring to put the Bible into the Kekchi language. Together they work long hours attempting to interpret the many clicks and grunts of the Kekchi into their first written language. When the missionary finds just the right word, the Kekchi smiles and nods vigorously. "It speaks to my heart," he says happily.

This young Indian working by the side of the consecrated missionary has spoken for all of us—the Bible *does* speak to our hearts, as it has spoken to the hearts of men and women down through the ages.

During the seventh century it spoke to the heart of the Venerable Bede as he lay desperately ill in a narrow cell in England. He would not give up to die until he had completed his translation of the Gospel of John so that others might read of God's redeeming love.

It spoke to the heart of John Wycliffe and gave him courage to stand trial before the archbishop of Canterbury and to endure hardship and persecution. Thus he was able to give to the world the first full translation of the Bible in the English language.

It spoke to the heart of Tyndale, who was burned at the stake for giving the world a clearer translation of the Bible.

The message of the Bible spoke to the heart of Robert Morrison. He spent 16 long years in a small, underground room in China in order to give the Chinese the Bible in their own language.

William Carey's heart heard the message and he endured poverty, personal loss, and hardship during the 40 years it took to put the Bible into the various languages of India.

Judson, the first American missionary to a foreign country, wasted away in a Burmese dungeon, his precious translation of the New Testament carefully hidden in his ragged pillow. It was Judson who gave to us these words of a hymn:

> *We love Thy name, we love Thy laws,*
> *And joyfully embrace Thy cause;*
> *We love Thy cross, the shame, the pain,*
> *O Lamb of God, for sinners slain.*

Henry Martyn burned his young life out in a few short years in the intense heat and long hours of labor required to put the Bible into the Arabic language.

The great open doors in Brazil today are possible only because Hugh Tucker spent many long years traveling up and down that country spreading Bibles and New Testament portions among the people. He bravely faced angry mobs, and asked only the privilege of telling of God's love as revealed through the Bible.

The Bible spoke to the heart of Esther Carson Winans and she gladly endured fever, exhaustion, persecution, and death. But she gave the Aguaruna Indians of

Peru their first written language in order that they might eventually have the Bible for their own.

It spoke to the hearts of five brave young missionaries some years ago. They gave their lives while attempting to contact the Aucas, a primitive tribe of head-hunting Indians in South America, in order to learn their language and eventually give them the Bible.

The Bible is speaking today to the hearts of many consecrated and gifted young people toiling among the obscure tribes of the world. These missionaries are working almost feverishly to translate the Bible into every known tongue.

But where are the John Wycliffes, the Robert Morrisons, the Judsons, and the Esther Carson Winanses of tomorrow—those whose hearts must be aflame with the love of God and His Word? Where are those who will go forth, not counting the cost, but giving themselves in full measure of devotion? They are the Rickys, the Cathys, the Michaels, and the Cindys of today—those eager-eyed youngsters in our homes and in the church school. It is up to us to inspire, to instruct, and to send them forth.

We must instill in these children a love for the Bible. We must help them to understand that it is the inspired Word of God; they must feel deeply that "the entrance of thy words giveth light" (Psalm 119:130).

Young people as never before need to be challenged with great and noble tasks. They need to be inspired to give their all. What greater task or challenge to their skills and intellects, their courage and ingenuity than to help in the great unfinished work of giving the Bible to the whole world?

Every child needs to know the love of God as revealed in the Bible. Every child needs to know the power of the gospel and the importance of the Bible as a Guide for daily living.

Basic Concepts

We may ask ourselves, What does the Bible tell us about God in simple, basic concepts that we can share with our children both in the home and in the church school?

1. *The Bible tells about God, the Creator.*

"In the beginning God created the heaven and the earth" (Genesis 1:1).

Thus the first verse in the Bible introduces us to God, who made our world. "All things were made by him; and without him was not any thing made that was made" (John 1:3).

This concept is most important when children ask *how* and *why*. It is important as never before when young minds are reaching out to grasp knowledge and scientific facts about the universe. What can be more important than that our children be rooted and grounded in the faith, "In the beginning God . . ."?

In this present-day search for knowledge of our world and the great expanse of space and its mysteries, it is most important that children have a growing concept of God. That concept must be adequate to meet all their searching and yearning for knowledge. Many young people have suffered a complete loss of faith during these critical years because their concept of God was not a growing one!

The greatest minds of all ages have been searching for answers—answers which God in His infinite wisdom has not yet revealed. What will be revealed through His providence and wisdom in the future we cannot know. But what we do not know, what we cannot understand, we accept and say with the writer to the Hebrews, "Through faith we understand that the worlds were framed by the word of God . . ." (Hebrews 11:3). We understand too that God is not limited by time and space and that one day is as a thousand years with the Lord, and a thousand years as one day. We remember the words of David: "For a thousand years in thy sight are but as yesterday when it is past, and as a watch in the night" (Psalm 90:4).

Another important truth to remember is that God did not create our world and then forget it. He set in motion the laws that govern life and He is deeply concerned and actively engaged in controlling the world that He has made. We see the wonders of His working powers round about us every day.

The Bible reveals to us in majestic language the greatness and power of God as revealed through His creative acts.

"O Lord my God, thou art very great; thou art clothed with honour and majesty" (Psalm 104:1).

"Oh that men would praise the Lord for his goodness, and for his wonderful works to the children of men!" (Psalm 107:8).

Children need to know more of the power and majesty of God. They need to be filled with a sense of wonder and awe as revealed through the majestic words of the Bible. Becoming familiar with some of these great passages and committing them to memory helps us to express our love and appreciation to God. It helps to increase our capacity for worship and praise to Him.

2. *The Bible tells about God's love.*

Throughout the Old and New Testaments we are told over and over again of the love of God. What a revelation of love we have in such tender passages as: ". . . I have loved thee with an everlasting love: . . ." (Jeremiah 31:3), and ". . . God so loved the world, that he gave his only begotten Son . . ." (John 3:16)!

While this plan of salvation is the supreme evidence of God's love, the Bible also reveals His love through His daily care and concern for us.

"The Lord is good to all: . . . ." (Psalm 145:9).

"Casting all your care upon him; for he careth for you" (1 Peter 5:7).

What assurance and comfort in these words for the troubled times in which we live! What a sense of security when we know not what the day will bring forth, to know that our Heavenly Father cares for us!

3. *The Bible tells that God is righteous.*

The Bible tells us over and over again of the righteousness of God.

"The Lord is righteous in all his ways, and holy in all his works" (Psalm 145:17).

Because God is a righteous God, He expects righteousness and obedience from us. It is the Bible that tells us what God expects of us.

4. *The Bible tells about Jesus, God's Son.*

God does not expect us to be righteous in our own strength. He has provided for us a way of salvation. It is the Bible that reveals to us His provision through His Son, Jesus Christ. It reveals to us the Living Word, the Lord Jesus, who lived, died, rose again, and someday will return.

The Gospel of John, chapter 1, declares to us the wonder of the Living Word.

"In the beginning was the Word, and the Word was with God, and the Word was God."

"In him was life; and the life was the light of men."

"And the Word was made flesh, and dwelt among us, (and we beheld his glory, the glory as of the only begotten of the Father,) full of grace and truth."

And in 1 John 1:1 we read:

"That which was from the beginning, which we have heard, which we have seen with our eyes, which we have looked upon, and our hands have handled, of the Word of life."

The Word of God made flesh, and dwelt among men! What a wonder! What a miracle that the Word of God was revealed through the lovely person of His Son, Jesus Christ! How difficult it is for our finite minds to grasp that holy wonder and meaning! And yet we have the testimony of an eyewitness, John the Beloved, that this is true.

"And we beheld his glory," the glory of the matchless Son of God. "That . . . which we have seen with our eyes"!

John had walked by the side of the Master on the dusty roads day by day. With his own eyes he had seen Jesus' loving acts of mercy, His tenderness and love. And John has given us in his Gospel a revelation of the tender, redeeming love of God.

The Bible, a Living Book

The Bible is a living Book. That is, it is a Guide to our daily living. How many times we turn to it for help and direction! We do not regard it as some magical device which will always open to the right spot when we need special help or guidance. But how often we do find help and direction as we read prayerfully, thoughtfully, searchingly, under the leadership of the Holy Spirit! Many times in rearing a family and in teaching children and young people we are asked, "Is this wrong? What should we do about this?" So often the Bible has the exact answer. There is direction, there is guidance in Philippians 4:8 and other passages.

". . . whatsoever things are true, whatsoever things are honest, whatsoever things are just, whatsoever things are pure, whatsoever things are lovely, whatsoever things are of good report; if there be any virtue, and if there be any praise, think on these things" (Philippians 4:8).

The Bible Helps Us Worship

The Bible is important as a language of worship. It helps us to express our feelings of joy and praise in the presence of God. It shows us how men through the ages have found expression for their highest and noblest aims and aspirations.

Many times when we have been looking at a gorgeous sunset with its rapidly changing hues of light these words have come to us to help us express our feelings:

> *The heavens declare the glory of God;*
> *and the firmament sheweth his handywork.*
> *Day unto day uttereth speech, and night*
> *unto night sheweth knowledge.*
> (Psalm 19:1-2)

Or when we watch a beautiful moth emerge from its dry cocoon to stretch forth its bright new wings in the sunlight, these words take on new beauty and meaning:

> *O Lord, how manifold are thy works!*
> *In wisdom hast thou made them all: the earth*
> *is full of thy riches.*
> *. . . Praise ye the Lord* (Psalm 104:24, 35).

Or as we ride through the countryside on an early morning in June, and see the rolling hills and fertile valleys stretched out before us, these words come with new meaning:

> *Thou crownest the year with thy goodness; . . .*
> *. . . the little hills rejoice on every side.*
> *The pastures are clothed with flocks; the valleys*
> *are also covered over with corn; they shout for*
> *joy, they also sing.*
> *Make a joyful noise unto God, all ye lands.*
> (Psalms 65:11-13; 66:1)

Yes, the Bible sets our hearts to singing in wonder and praise as we think of the goodness of God.

The Bible Is a Source of Comfort

The Bible is a source of comfort in time of sorrow and trouble, even down to the shadow of death. I stood beside the bedside of my mother in the last hours of her life. Hers had been a lifetime of following God in joyful, consecrated service. There had been many trials through the years, but the joy of the Lord was her strength. The Bible was always a great source of comfort and she read and committed many passages to memory. Now the end was much nearer than I dreamed as I held her hand and read to her Psalm 27:

> *"The Lord is my light and my salvation; whom shall I fear?*
> *the Lord is the strength of my life; of whom shall I be afraid? . . .*
> *For in the time of trouble he shall hide me in his pavilion: . . .*
> *I had fainted, unless I had believed to see the goodness*
> *of the Lord in the land of the living.*
> *Wait on the Lord: be of good courage . . ."*

When the psalm was finished, Mother said, "That is all I need." Those were her last words to me . . . words of victory and triumph over death itself. Before morning she was in the presence of the Living Word.

Yes, through joy and sorrow the Bible speaks to our hearts. It is a Lamp unto our feet and a Light unto our paths. No wonder we love it. No wonder we teach it diligently to our children in accordance with the Word itself:

"And these words, which I command thee this day, shall be in thine heart:

"And thou shalt teach them diligently unto thy children, and shalt talk of them when thou sittest in thine house, and when thou walkest by the way, and when thou liest down, and when thou risest up" (Deuteronomy 6:7).

PART TWO:

Before We Can Share the Bible

Before we can share the Bible with our children, we ourselves must understand some things about God's Word. It must be a living Book to us, one that speaks to our own hearts with truth and power. Two were walking along the Emmaus way with the Living Word one day, and said later, "Did not our heart burn within us, while he talked with us by the way, and while he opened to us the scriptures?" Our own hearts, like theirs, must burn with love and conviction as we read and study the Bible.

It is not necessary for us to be profound scholars before we can teach the Bible to our children. That of course is impractical. But every sincere Christian who undertakes to teach others needs to know what the Bible is about.

The Structure and Theme of the Bible

We need to have a good general knowledge of the structure and theme of the Bible. We need to understand something of how God has revealed himself through the different books of the Bible, and how to relate the various parts of the Bible to the central theme. We need to know something of the times when the various books were written, and the social and economic background of the peoples of those times.

There are many good books and commentaries to help the earnest teacher and parent to know more about the Bible. (See "For Further Study.") Some of these books should be a part of each family and church library.

As we begin to understand something of the general plan and theme of the Bible, it will unfold to us in a thrilling way. The theme of the Bible is God's redeeming love, our gift of eternal life through His Son, Jesus Christ. The plan of the Bible is the account of God's patient dealing with man to bring about His supreme purpose of redemption.

As we study the Bible, it becomes clear to us that the Old Testament sets forth the long preparation and looking forward to the coming of God's Son as the Redeemer of the world. The New Testament is an account of the coming of the Redeemer and His work. Through the Gospels and the Book of Acts we feel that we too are eyewitnesses to His glory and partakers of the joy and wonder of the apostles. As we read in the Old Testament the sad accounts of the backslidings and failures of God's people, we cry out with the prophets, How long, O God, how long, until the Redeemer will come?

The Bible is composed of 66 books with many different writers from different times and circumstances, yet there is beautiful unity and harmony throughout. We may see in each book its own distinct purpose within the general theme and plan. This unity is apparent in the first and last verses of the Bible: "In the beginning God . . . ," and the last verse deals with man: "The grace of our Lord Jesus Christ be with you all." The story between these two verses is the absorbing account of God's loving, seeking, and redeeming man from sin.

The Old Testament

The Book of Genesis is the book of beginnings, the

beginning of the universe, the beginning of man, the beginning of sin, and the beginning of God's redemption. The Book of Revelation tells of our ultimate destiny with our Lord: "I am the beginning and the end."

Someone has said that the Bible is God's picture album, in which He pictures sinners and saints exactly as they were. We see, too, different pictures of God as revealed through the picture portraits, particularly in the Old Testament.

In the story of Moses and the books of law we see the God of Sinai. These books reveal to us God's uncompromising dealing with sin. He said to His people, "Thou shalt not," because rebellious, wandering Israel needed most of all to learn obedience. But the story of Moses also reveals to us God's loving care and protection of His people.

In the Major Prophets, God reveals himself in various ways. Strange as it may seem, we learn through the fiery prophet Elijah that God reveals himself, not through the whirlwind, but through the still, small voice—His Spirit dealing with our spirits. The prophet Isaiah reveals the majesty and power of God. His message points us forward to the coming of the Messiah.

Who can read the words, "Comfort ye, comfort ye my people," without rejoicing in God's tenderness and love? Can we read, "Who hath believed our report? and to whom is the arm of the Lord revealed?" without thrilling to the joy of God's redeeming grace?

The Minor Prophets also reveal pictures of God. Amos shows the divine demand for justice, and Hosea tells of God's love and mercy toward the backslider.

The books of poetry—Psalms, Songs of Solomon, Lamentations, Proverbs, Job, Ecclesiastes—are designed to deepen the devotional life and give us a language of worship. Some of the great truths of the Bible are expressed in beautiful poetic language. Much of the majesty and greatness of God is set forth in these writings.

O sing unto the Lord a new song: . . .
Give unto the Lord the glory due unto his name: . . .
O worship the Lord in the beauty of holiness: . . .
Let the heavens rejoice, and let the earth be glad; . . .

(Psalm 96)

Malachi closes the Old Testament with the glorious hope of the coming Messiah, the "Sun of righteousness."

The New Testament

The New Testament gives us an eyewitness account of the coming of the Messiah. In the sublime story of the Babe of Bethlehem the Old Testament prophecy is wonderfully fulfilled: "Unto us a child is born, unto us a son is given."

In the New Testament we find the same unity and harmony as the various books fit together to give us a complete picture of the fulfillment of God's plan of salvation. As the Old Testament foretells Christ the Messiah, the New Testament reveals Jesus as Saviour.

Matthew, the first book of the New Testament, was written to the Jewish people and thus portrays Christ the King. It tells us the story of the kings of the East coming to worship the newborn King at Bethlehem. In Matthew 21:5 we read of Jesus: "Behold, thy king cometh . . ."

The Book of Mark is written to the Romans and tells of Jesus as the Servant and Son of God. ". . . the Son of man came not to be ministered unto, but to minister . . ." (Mark 10:45). It is a book of action given in crisp, concise words.

Luke writes to the Greeks and presents our Lord as the universal Christ who came to save all (Luke 19:10).

The Gospel of John is written primarily to Christians and tells of the deity of Christ (John 1:14).

The Book of Acts, written by Luke, is a bridge between the Gospels and the Epistles. It tells how the disciples went forth to carry out the Great Commission. Its pages glow with the joy and enthusiasm of the early Christians as they set forth to do His will in the face of suffering, hardships, and death.

The Epistles were written to interpret the Gospels and to teach us how to live the Christian life.

"And whatsoever ye do in word or deed, do all in the name of the Lord Jesus, giving thanks to God and the Father by him" (Colossians 3:17).

What the Bible Means to Us

As we think of teaching the Bible to children, we must ask ourselves how we can use it in our own lives. Do we read it daily for help and guidance? Do we ask the Holy Spirit to help us appropriate its instructions and promises to our own experiences? Do we find comfort and help from its matchless words? Do we want to share its message with others?

It is only as we love and use the Bible ourselves that we will be able to share it fully with our children. It is only as the teachings of the Bible are reflected in our own lives that the children will be attracted to its message and teaching.

O Word of God incarnate,
O wisdom from on high,
O truth unchanged, unchanging,
O light of our dark sky;
We praise thee for the radiance
That from the hallowed page,

A lantern to our footsteps,
Shines on from age to age.
—WILLIAM H. HOW

The Laws of Learning

Before we can share the Bible with children either in the home or in the church school, we need to know something of the laws of learning.

The Bible itself gives us the key to effective teaching by presenting to us the world's greatest Teacher, the Lord Jesus. From Him we may learn the most effective ways of teaching. He knew the laws of learning. He knew His pupils and He knew the Scriptures. He constantly used scripture verses to tell about God and to enrich His teaching. In His childhood He had learned many stories of men of old who loved and served God bravely. He had learned the law of Moses. He had committed many passages to memory and He quoted from these continuously as He taught. He began His preaching ministry reading from the prophet Isaiah: "The Spirit of the Lord is upon me, because he hath anointed me to preach the gospel to the poor; . . ." (Luke 4:18). His last words upon the Cross were quoted from the Psalms: ". . . into thy hands I commend my spirit: . . ." (See Luke 23:4*b* and Psalm 31:5.)

1. *The law of readiness*

Jesus exemplified this important law in all His teaching. He understood the capacities of those He taught and did not go beyond. Sometimes He refrained from teaching certain truths because of the emotional, mental, and spiritual limitations of those He taught. He was the Source of all truth. He knew all the wonders of science and the mysteries of the origin of life. He was present when the worlds were formed and helped in the act of creation. "All things were made by him; and without him was not any thing made that was made" (John 1:3). Yet we have no record of Him discussing these things with the humble fishermen. "I have yet many things to say unto you," He said, "but ye cannot bear them now" (John 16:12). So He spoke to them of catching fish, of wind and sun and rain—things which they knew and could understand.

Jesus used the language of His pupils. He used terms and words which were familiar to those He taught, He used simple expressions—short, meaningful words.

Learning is possible only when the person is ready to learn. As teachers of children, we want to be sure the child is ready to accept what we teach. If we spend too much time drilling a child on mere facts of the Bible or in learning long passages which are beyond his capacity, we violate the law of readiness. We may thus do great damage to the child's future enjoyment and desire to know more about the Bible. For this reason, selecting graded biblical material is important in teaching children. We do not try to teach nursery children Bible material that is suitable only for children of junior age. We do not use long theological terms which are beyond the interest and understanding of the young child.

2. *The law of practice*

We learn by doing. Jesus often told pupils to put His teaching immediately into practice. "Go, and do thou likewise." "Stretch forth thy hand." "Go, wash in the pool of Siloam."

Truths which are put into practice immediately are long remembered.

Jesus said, "This is my commandment, That ye love one another." So we provide experiences of showing love, sharing, helping one another, in order that children may do what Jesus said and learn the true meaning of this verse.

3. *The law of feeling or satisfaction*

Jesus sent out His disciples to preach, teach, and heal as He had taught them. The Bible says that after they had done these things they returned with joy. They were ready to do these things again. That is what we mean by feeling or satisfaction.

When a Bible truth has been learned and then put into practice (such as a sharing project for the children), the joy that follows convinces the child that what he was told is true. When we teach a child the verse, "If ye love me, keep my commandments," we urge him to keep Christ's commandments. We do this because we know there is joy and satisfaction in putting into practice what Jesus taught. We do this because we know the child will remember what he has enjoyed.

The Ways in Which Children Learn

1. *Learning through the senses: seeing, hearing, smelling, touching, tasting*

Jesus taught through the senses. He called attention to the songs of the birds, the flowers blooming on the hillsides, and the wind touching their cheeks. In so doing, no doubt He called from His store of happy childhood experiences of playing on the sunny hillsides around Nazareth, where He grew and increased in "wisdom and stature, and in favour with God and man" (Luke 2:52).

When we take children out of doors to observe the creative works of God, we are teaching them Bible truths through all their senses. We increase their capacity for worship and response to God, and we lay a firm foundation for true fellowship with God.

The child who sees the beauty of a rose, touches its velvety petals, and smells its delicate fragrance, learns in unforgettable ways of the wonder and love of God when interpreted in the light of the Bible verse: "He hath made every thing beautiful..." (Ecclesiastes 3:11).

Sally, as a four-year-old, was having such an experience. "Oh, I just love God for giving us such beautiful roses!" she said reverently. Today she is a primary teacher in the Sunday school, teaching other children about God's love. (She is also president of her garden club!)

2. *Learning through curiosity*

How often Jesus used the curiosity of His listeners to spark their interest in what He wanted to teach them! Sometimes He did it with a lead question such as, "What man of you, having a hundred sheep, . . . ?" (Luke 15:4) Sometimes He used objects to catch attention, "Shew me a penny." He knew that, before He could teach, He must have attention.

It is important for us to know too that a child's curiosity helps him to learn. His eagerness to know the *how* and *why*, his interest in the things about him, provide many opportunities for teaching. That is why it is important in our teaching to provide experiences with interesting things to arouse curiosity and to provide readiness for learning.

3. *Learning by association*

Often Jesus related new truths to that which was already familiar. To the woman who came to draw water, He spoke of the living water. To the farmer, He talked about sowing seed. To the shepherd, He told the story of the lost sheep.

When we try to teach the Bible apart from the world in which the child lives, it is an obscure and uninteresting Book to them. But children love familiar things. They love familiar songs and stories. They love the things they know and use each day. So when we want to teach them a Bible truth, we try to associate it with something familiar to them.

4. *Learning through a variety of methods*

Jesus was a master Storyteller but He did not rely on this method alone in teaching. He used all the methods at His disposal that were suitable with those He sought to teach.

Often teachers greatly limit their teaching through a sameness of method. In teaching the Bible we want first of all to spark the children's interest, and then to inspire them to learn and to start their quest with eagerness. We need to use all the teaching tools and methods at our disposal to make that quest interesting and challenging along the way.

5. *Learning through imitation*

Jesus often dramatized His teaching by showing His disciples what He wanted them to do. He washed His disciples' feet to teach them humility. He rode a colt into the city to teach His kingship.

Children readily imitate that which they admire. This desire to imitate is a valuable tool in teaching. Dramatizing a story is one of the best means of helping a child to know what it is like to be brave, responsible, honest, and helpful.

> *There was a child went forth every day*
> *and the first object he look'd upon,*
> *that object he became,*
> *And that object became part of him for*
> *the day or a certain part of the day,*
> *or for many years or stretching*
> *cycles of years.**

6. *Learning through activities*

This reminds us how Jesus gave His disciples some-

---

*From "There Was a Child Went Forth," *Leaves of Grass,* by Walt Whitman (New York: Doubleday & Company, Inc., 1924). Used by permission.

thing to do to carry out what He taught them. He knew the importance of activity in the learning process.

Activities are an important part of the child's learning. The things he does, his experiences with others, giving, sharing, helping, all help him to learn to live successfully in the world about him.

When children work and plan together, when they accept responsibility and carry out their plans successfully, they are learning important ways of living according to Bible truths.

Creative activities bring satisfaction and a means of self-expression to children. Such activities help them to feel a fellowship with God, the Creator of all.

All activities of course must be suited to the child's age and abilities and therefore will be discussed at length in later chapters dealing with specific age-groups.

7. *Learning through insight*

Jesus said, "I thank thee, O Father, . . . because thou hast hid these things from the wise and prudent, and hast revealed them unto babes" (Matthew 11:25).

Insight is that God-given something inside children that helps them to learn what we are trying to teach. Often God seems to whisper in their hearts and gives them understanding beyond their years. Children vary of course, depending somewhat upon home environment and training, but all of us are amazed at times at the spiritual insight of the children we teach.

The Teacher

As we think about how Jesus taught, we remember one more important truth—the *teacher* is more than the lesson. Jesus was everything that He taught. He was always tender, loving, sympathetic, kind, and gracious. His manner was earnest and unhurried. He always kept His poise.

Does this say something to us as teachers when we come before our children on Sunday morning ill at ease and unprepared? We need to be efficient without becoming professional. We need to be kind without being apologetic. We need to be warm and enthusiastic without being effusive. We need to be easy and natural in our manner and yet inspire reverence. Let us pray that in these things too we may ever be like the Master!

> *Oh, to be like Thee! blessed Redeemer,*
> *This is my constant longing and prayer.*
> *Gladly I'll forfeit all of earth's treasures,*
> *Jesus, Thy perfect likeness to wear.*
> —T. O. CHISHOLM

FOR STUDY AND DISCUSSION

1. Discuss three reasons why we should share the Bible with our children.

2. List three devotional passages which have been a source of comfort and help to you. Could any of these be used successfully with children?

3. Tell what your church does to help parents share the Bible with children in the home.

4. List four ways in which we can teach as Jesus taught.

5. Describe an activity which you have used to help children learn a Bible verse or Bible truth.

FOR FURTHER STUDY

Halley's Bible Handbook (new revised edition)
Exploring the Old Testament, edited by W. T. Purkiser
Exploring the New Testament, edited by Ralph Earle
Bible Encyclopedia for Children, by Cecil Northcutt
The Golden Bible Atlas, by Samuel Terrien, Golden Press
Everyday Life in Bible Times, National Geographic

2/

*Oh, teach me, Lord, that I may teach
 The precious things Thou dost impart,
And wing my words that they may reach
 The hidden depths of many a heart.*
—Frances Havergal

Rightly Dividing the Word of Truth

The Teacher and the Task

When the Bible is a real and living Book to the teacher, when teachers understand the ways in which children learn, then they turn to the task itself.

How shall I make the Bible real to the children I teach? the sincere teacher asks.

The good teacher knows that the most effective way of teaching the Bible is not only through the telling of Bible stories and the teaching of a Bible memory verse. The Bible story and the Bible memory verse are important. However, the teacher must constantly seek interesting ways of making these stories and verses live for the children. Plans must be made to provide rich and varied experiences with the use of the Bible. A variety of methods and good materials with which to work are also important.

Purpose

Before considering methods and materials for use in teaching the Bible, the teacher must understand the

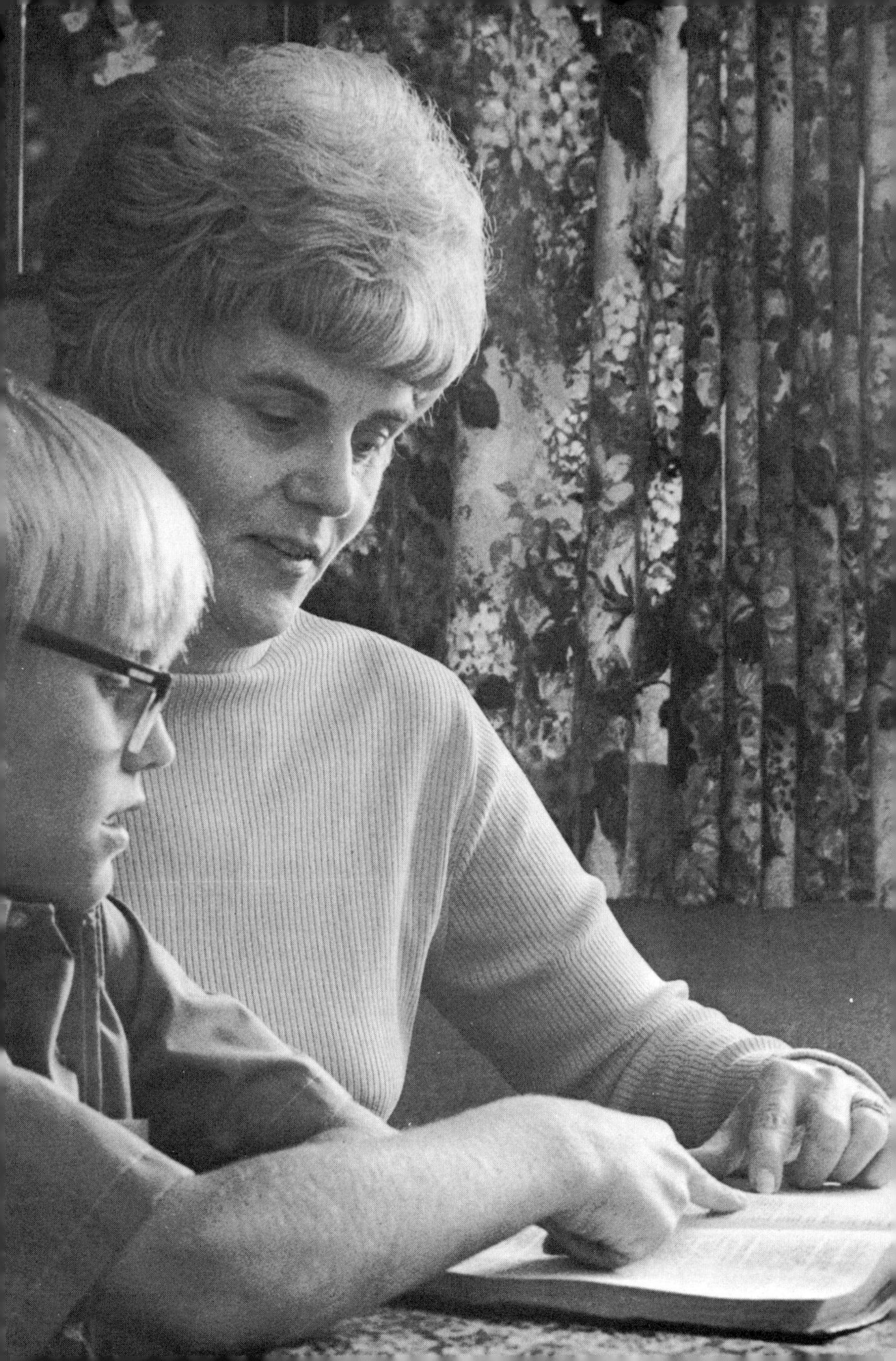

purpose clearly. These questions should be asked: How can my teaching of the Bible help the children to know and love God? How can I lead them into an understanding of God's plan of salvation as revealed in the Bible? How can I teach them to love and appreciate the Bible, and to learn to turn to it for guidance and help in daily living? How can I lay foundations that will bring them to a love for the Lord Jesus, and a commitment of their lives to Him?

The curriculum materials of the Sunday school are carefully planned with these purposes in mind. Therefore the teacher turns first to the lesson materials. The purpose for each unit and session are carefully studied before attempting to teach.

With the purposes well in mind, the teacher turns to a consideration of materials and methods suitable to the age-group with which he/she works.

Methods and Materials

In addition to the curriculum materials and the Bible itself, the teacher will need a good concordance and books about the Bible. Books about customs and ways of living in Bible times, maps, and other resource material are of great value in giving the teacher a working knowledge of the Bible.

Books on creative activities, how to make and do, religious and public school periodicals are invaluable in helping the teacher learn new ways of making her teaching interesting and effective. (See "For Further Study" at the end of chapter.)

Pictures, poems, books for children, and objects of interest will greatly enrich use of the Bible. In planning activities and experiences for the children, the teacher will think of making charts, outlines, and posters according to the ability and interest to the children. Plans will be made to lead them in creating murals, friezes, rebuses, and maps as an outgrowth of their experience and learnings. The quest for Bible knowledge will be made interesting through the use of riddles, puzzles, quizzes, games, research, and reports.

Bible stories will come alive through good telling, and with dramatization and role playing. Peep boxes will make Bible scenes live in the child's memory. And through it all the teacher will enrich his/her teaching with singing of Bible verses, choral readings, and using Bible passages with the children.

The teacher will seek to provide experiences whereby the children may put into practice the Bible verses they learn.

The Creative Teacher

What do we mean by a creative teacher? It will help us to think again of the ways Jesus taught, for He was a creative Teacher. He used many methods and gave His pupils something to do to put their learning into practice. He directed the thinking of His pupils and led them to find for themselves the answers to their questions.

The creative teacher of children is eager and ready to learn and try new methods of teaching the Bible. The teacher directs the children into activities but does not dictate to them step by step what to do. The children are regarded as the greatest resource. What rewarding times are enjoyed by pupil and teacher alike through conversation, planning, and working together! The children's responses, their eagerness to learn, their insight into spiritual truths, their fresh approach, and their ability to achieve all bring richness to the teaching experience.

The creative teacher seeks to help the child relate the Bible to life experiences so that it will become a Guidebook for daily living. What earnest Christian has not sought such help consistently, especially in time of need?

Recently when distressed over circumstances beyond my control, I opened my Bible for help and guidance. There a verse I no doubt had read many times spoke clearly to me in gentle rebuke. "And let the peace of God rule in your hearts, . . . and be ye thankful" (Colossians 3:15). I began to count my blessings and found comfort and peace. I had related a Bible verse to my own need. The child needs to learn very early in life that right choices may be made through turning to the Bible for light and guidance.

Let's Try Creative Teaching

When we realize the importance of creative teaching, why are we so timid about attempting it with our children? Why are we afraid to try new methods and new ways of teaching the Bible? Why do we hesitate to undertake creative activities? Perhaps it is because many of us were not taught creatively. Perhaps we have tried creative methods with our group and have failed.

"I asked my pupils to do creative drawings," said an earnest teacher, "but they just sat and looked at me!"

Another teacher attempted a springtime frieze with her class of five-year-olds. "Draw pictures about spring," she said hopefully. But the spring was late that year. Snow was on the ground that Sunday morning. There were no evidences of spring outdoors or in the room. Why should the children draw pictures of something they did not feel? No wonder they sat at the table looking bewildered. One little girl wanted to cooperate and please her teacher, so she drew a picture of a Japanese cherry tree with blossoms on it. (The class had just completed a missionary study on Japan.) Otherwise the group was sterile, and the teacher said later, "I just can't teach that way."

This brings us to an important prerequisite for creative activities, whether it be drawing, painting, writing, or other creative work. The children must *feel* what they do. They must be motivated by things they see, feel, hear, touch. There must be rich and vivid experiences to inspire them. They must *feel* if they are to express themselves creatively.

But how do we stimulate these feelings? How do we provide these experiences which make children feel and want to express?

The type of experience of course depends upon what we are trying to do. If we want to teach them about God, the Creator, firsthand experiences in the out-of-doors—trips, hikes, or just a walk around the block for the very young child—help him to feel and to know that God is great and good. If we want to teach the verse, "[Jesus said,] . . . love one another, as I have loved you" (John 15:12), we provide a sharing experience where the child may show love to someone.

Stories of Bible people become real when children build a Palestinian village or a shepherd scene and learn ways and customs of these people.

Thinking creatively through the planning of charts, maps, and reports adds interest and stimulation to the child's quest for knowledge of the Bible.

Creative activities such as painting, drawing, and the making of murals, friezes, and posters are happy, satisfying experiences for children in their exploration of the facts and truths of the Bible. To know how to plan a mural or frieze accurately, the child must learn facts and gather information which he will long remember. There is genuine satisfaction in using these facts creatively to share with others. It also satisfies the child's need for self-expression.

The teacher who said her children only "sat and looked at her" was willing to try again. After a Saturday trip to the country, she brought an interesting collection of seed pods, leaves, nuts, and other things to Sunday school on Sunday morning. There were also pictures and books to illustrate the fall season. There were poems attractively mounted. When the children came, their interest was aroused at once. The teacher directed the conversation into talking about God's plan in autumn. Bible verses were looked up and read together.

"Let's sing our song about God making our world," said one little girl. "God, Who Made the World of Beauty" was sung with meaning and reverence.

"Perhaps you would like to draw pictures of some of the beautiful things God has made," suggested the teacher.

There were drawings of trees, birds, leaves, sun, and rain.

"Why can't we put our pictures up on the wall for everyone to see?" said John.

"We can," said the teacher. A strip of shelf paper was provided, and the pictures pasted on.

"What shall we write at the top?" asked the teacher.

Several suggestions were made and finally the words,

"Thank You, God," were printed at the top.

"Should we print our Bible verse at the bottom?" asked the teacher. And this verse was added: "O give thanks unto the Lord; for he is good."

At the close of the session the children looked at the beautiful frieze they had created, read the Bible verse together, and stood in a semicircle, heads bowed, for a closing prayer of thanks.

We recognize two important facts about creative activities from this teacher's experience. First of all, she provided materials to stimulate the child's interest so there would be a desire to create. Secondly, when the child was ready, there were materials to work with.

We will observe also that in this case the teacher made suggestions but did not tell the children what to do.

For primary and older elementary children, ongoing activities that continue for several Sundays are more valuable than the isolated Sunday-by-Sunday projects. It is important that the pupils understand what they are doing and help to plan.

Suppose a primary group decides to make a table scene of the story of Abraham. There will be a discussion first of what such a scene would include, how the people lived, what the tents were made of, how the people made a living, and how they dressed. A chart would be made of things the pupils needed to know before such a scene could be started. Committees could be appointed to find the answers through pictures, books, and conversation, and report back to the group. The materials needed and the type of figures to be made would be discussed before any actual work was begun. Thus it becomes the children's own project. When the project is completed, there needs to be evaluation by the children themselves and a sharing of their work with others.

Almost every type of making and doing can be used

effectively in teaching the Bible to children. Not all types of activities are suitable for Sunday morning, but vacation Bible school affords rich opportunity for projects requiring more time and manual labor.

These are excellent books (see "For Further Study") to help the teacher and parent learn how to make and use dioramas (see page 116), murals, picture reels (see page 92), table scenes, peep boxes (see page 94), illustrated charts, and posters. Other fascinating ways of teaching the Bible to children at home and in the church school are also discussed.

Is the use of prepared handwork or an activity packet considered creative teaching? It can be if it is planned that way. It needs to be creative in its suggestions, and have a wide variety and scope. It must enrich the unit of study and carry out some thought or interpretation of truth. Prepared handwork may also be valuable in increasing a child's knowledge of Bible background, living conditions, habits, and customs of Bible times.

Pictures

Pictures are invaluable for teaching the Bible to children. They furnish information about homes, clothing, customs, and ways of living during Bible times. They tell the story of how our Bible came to us down through the ages.

Pictures supplied with lesson materials help to make Bible stories live for the children. They help the children visualize the characters, setting, and action. Symbolic pictures should usually not be used with children younger than junior age.

Pictures lead to conversation, and conversation to search for knowledge.

Pictures teach Bible truths and stimulate good behavior. They create atmosphere and lead to worship.

They may prepare the way for a prayer, a song, or verses from the Bible.

Permanent pictures in the home and church school are important. They should be chosen wisely. In some cities, pictures may be checked out of the public library for several weeks at a time. The *Sistine Madonna, Madonna of the Chair,* and other famous pictures are particularly useful during the Christmas season.

Audiovisual Aids

Other visual aids such as filmstrips and slides are most effective in teaching the Bible to children. These materials contain valuable information regarding Bible lands, customs, and people, and thus help the children to feel at home with the Bible. Films and filmstrips regarding the story of our Bible, how it came to be and how it is being circulated and used around the world today, are available for use in the home and church school.

Cassettes, Show'N Tell, and View-Masters also provide interesting Bible stories and materials. Information regarding such material is available from the audiovisual department of your publishing house.

Dramatization

Dramatization—acting out Bible stories—is another effective and interesting way of making the Bible live for children. Beginning with the very young child who lives in a world of play, through primary and junior years, playing a story is a valuable tool.

Those of us who have lived with children in the home know that many times the living room is not a living room at all—it is a deep, deep forest with bears and tigers roaming about. The dining room table is a tent where people live. Mother must watch for pans of water put out for the lions and tigers.

This love of play-acting can be used effectively in the church school. Children are not apt to forget stories when they have planned to share them with others through dramatization. The teacher who opens this magic door needs to know something about it in order to make it the enriching experience that it can be. Reading a good book on creative drama with children will be most helpful. (See "For Further Study.") Before the children can play a story, it must be thoroughly familiar to them. The story with action, direct discourse, and a real message is best suited to dramatization. Children need to have a part in planning, what costumes (if any), what properties, and what the conversation will be. Dramatization should be spontaneous, natural, without any thought of perfection or a finished production.

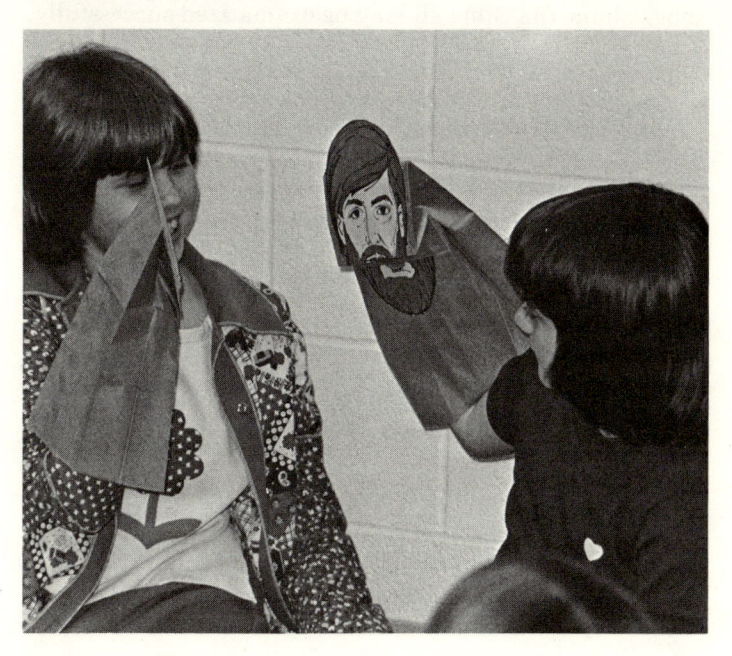

Pantomime, tableau, and picture posing are also instructive and interesting to children.

Play-acting may sometimes take the form of creating puppets to use in retelling a story. There are many interesting ways of making puppets: hand puppets, finger puppets, paper bags, and stick puppets, all of which children love to make and use.

Making small figures and manipulating them on a table, bench, or in a box are interesting and helpful. These may be made from paper, clay, craft wire, and clothespins. The peep box, the *kamishibai* (Japanese story box), and the story picture reel may be used to recall Bible stories and to teach Bible truths.

What shall we dramatize? Bible stories, stories that illustrate Bible truths, Christmas carols, Bible songs, and songs about the Bible all may be dramatized successfully.

Games

The use of games as a learning procedure is becoming more popular both in secular schools and in Christian education. It is a highly successful method and one by which children learn readily. Such games are used not to entertain but to communicate Bible facts, to change attitudes, and to develop skills in use of the Bible.

Games may be used to introduce a unit of study and to create interest. They may also be used during the unit or at the close to review what has been learned. They are effective in helping children learn or recall Bible memory verses. Games may help to clarify concepts and reveal what the children are thinking and feeling. Bible games may be used to involve the children in the learning process.

Games help the child to build selfconfidence while he is learning important facts and truths.

Many types of games are recommended and provided

through the curriculum materials. These vary according to the age-group and skills of the children involved. Well-known games such as Ticktacktoe and Concentration may be adapted to learning Bible facts and concepts. Interesting Bible games may also be obtained through bookstores and from your publishing house.

The Use of Creative Writing

Creative writing is an interesting and effective Bible teaching tool. Children may learn to express their thoughts about God, Jesus, and the Bible through prayers, poems, stories, and sentences for scrapbooks or script for plays.

Young children often express their thoughts creatively before they are old enough to record them. When our children were very young, I was amazed by their ability to express themselves creatively. Often I wished for a pencil to record them, but to make a move would have broken the magic spell. Among our family treasures are notes in which the children themselves recorded their thoughts just for fun when they thought no one was looking. I have notes in childish scrawl entitled "About My Mother," "Our President," "A Robin," and others.

When Phyllis was a very little girl, she said, "I know a story but I can't spell the words." (She really couldn't write yet.)

"I will help you," her mother said, and wrote down the little story as she dictated it. When the story was written, Phyllis showed it to her daddy, who promptly drew a picture to go with it. That night Phyllis went to bed with the story under her pillow and the picture on her wall nearby.

While the home is the most fruitful place for creative writing, often one creative child in a church school class will spark the entire group to write something truly beautiful.

A springtime prayer may be a group project:

Thank You, God, for springtime;
For flowers, birds, and trees,
For sunshine and the raindrops—
Thank You, God, for these.

Such a poem need not rhyme but sometimes it does. When the words have been printed on a chart or poster, pictures may be drawn in place of the nouns to make a rebus. A Bible verse may be added. It is a rewarding experience for teacher and pupils.

Older children may write stories of their own about Bible passages. After reading a passage to children and discussing it with them, you may say, "How do you think people felt when Jesus said, 'If ye love me, keep my commandments'? Can you write a story about someone showing love for one another as Jesus said?" Children may also be asked to retell Bible stories in their own words. They may write stories of how our Bible came to us or stories of people who knew and loved the Bible.

Storytelling

Storytelling is and always will be an important tool in teaching the Bible to children. They are always ready for a good story, and a good story will do what nothing else can do. A story may be used to inform, enlighten, change attitudes and behavior, teach Bible truths, inspire, and lead to worship.

Every good story has four well-defined parts—an introduction, body, or development, climax, and conclusion. The good story catches attention at once and goes somewhere. It presents problems to solve and difficulties to overcome. It has direct discourse and crisp, vivid words.

Look at the stories Jesus told. He caught attention

at once; He introduced His characters forthwith; He presented the plot or problems, carried the theme to a climax, and left a satisfactory conclusion.

Bible stories as given in the lesson materials are usually well written and interesting. Sometimes the teacher feels the story needs to be expanded to add interest. How far shall we go? Is it all right to use our imagination in supplying details?

A good rule in expanding Bible stories either for writing or telling is this: Details may be supplied to make the story more interesting when these details are in keeping with known facts about the customs and habits of Bible people. Direct discourse is always to be preferred where the conversation is implied in the text.

When we write or tell stories about Jesus as a boy, we can be sure by verses given us in the Bible that He was helpful, obedient, and good. When we tell stories about Him helping His parents, it is well to remind the children the Bible does not actually relate this, but because we know He was good and obedient, we know He helped. We know He undoubtedly went to synagogue school as other boys, and lived a happy, normal life. We know this because of what we know of Jewish life in those days, and because of what Jesus was as an adult.

Not all Bible stories are suitable for children. Some are difficult even for adults to understand fully. Children do not have the mature judgment and understanding to get a clear picture of God from the telling of some of the stories. Therefore we choose those stories within the understanding of sensitive young minds. We ask ourselves, too: What is the purpose of this story? Does it help the child to have a clearer picture of God? Does it reveal spiritual truths which have real value to the child in his present stage of development?

When we have chosen our story, we should prepare

it carefully. Know the four parts of the story. Have a good beginning and a satisfactory ending. Present your problems and let your characters move at once. Know where you climax is and plan to let your listeners know by the tone of your voice as you tell. Now practice your story. Say it to yourself and to anyone else who will listen. One primary teacher who felt she needed an audience for practicing her story arranged pictures of her family on the sofa in the living room. Sitting before the pictures as she would a group of children, she practiced. When she told the story later to her children, they were delighted with her ease and skill.

When you tell a story, be alive every second. Avoid repetition and useless description. And when you are through—stop. Don't ruin your story by added explanations and moralizing. If it is a good story well told, the children will get the point and make the application themselves.

Choral Speaking

Choral speaking—the group reading together—is valuable in teaching older primary and junior children. It is a wonderful way to teach appreciation of some of the great passages of the Bible. It is interesting to them to know that people long ago used choral speaking in their worship. Children find joy in using this ancient art for expressing their thoughts of worship.

Some of the psalms, the Christmas story (Luke 2:8-20), Matthew 5:1-16, and others may be used successfully. Poems about the Bible or Bible truths may be used with younger children. The selections to be used may be printed on the blackboard or large sheet of paper. As the children become familiar with the material, they decide themselves how it is to be spoken. Then the pattern is marked by lines.

Children enjoy using choral readings especially during the worship service or on special days such as Christmas and Thanksgiving.

Sharing the Bible Through Music

This is my Father's world,
And to my list'ning ears,
All nature sings, and round me rings
The music of the spheres.
—MALTBIE D. BABCOCK

The world that God has created for us is full of music. We can hear it all about us if we listen. It is one of the "all things" that God has given us richly to enjoy.

Music is as old as the world itself, for we read in the Book of Job how the morning stars sang together when the foundations of the earth were laid (Job 38:4, 7). It has been used down through the ages to express man's hopes, joys, aspirations, and dreams. It has been used to lift men into active fellowship with our Lord. God has given us music that we might express our love and praise to Him.

"Why do you always write such lively religious music?" someone asked the famous composer Haydn.

"I cannot help it," said Haydn. "Whenever I think of God, my heart is so full of joy, my fingers fairly run up and down the keyboard. I must write joyful music when I think about God."

It was Haydn who gave us the joyful hymn "O Worship the King," to help us express our joy and praise to God.

The Bible, too, is filled with music. Many of its beautiful passages sing their way into our hearts and help us give praise and thanks to God. The Bible has also been a source of inspiration for much of the world's finest music.

Music plays a most important part in our use of the

Bible with children. Children thrill to the musical words and the rhythmic pattern of some of the selections we use in worship. They enjoy singing Bible verses, and it is a most effective way of teaching the verses we want them to remember.

Good songs are most helpful in teaching children the important truths about God and Jesus. Bible truths contained in such songs are long remembered by the children.

Whenever we use a song or chorus about the Bible, we need to be sure that the words and music are worthy of teaching about God and His Word. We need to ask ourselves, Does this chorus or song increase the child's appreciation for the Bible? Are the words within the understanding of the age-group with which it is being used? Does it picture a true concept of God and the Lord Jesus? Are the children likely to form any hazy or confusing ideas from its usage? Are the words trivial and lacking in real meaning? We need to consider the music too. Is it more than just a catchy tune? Does it tend to increase the child's feeling of worship?

In the Home

Music may be used in the home to teach a child about God, Jesus, and the Bible.

While the child is still very young, this beautiful little song can help him to understand that God made all things:

> *Oh, who can make a flower?*
> *I'm sure I can't, can you?*
> *Oh, who can make a flower?*
> *No one but God, 'tis true.*[*]
>
> GRACE W. OWENS

Such a song prepares a child's thinking for a later learning

---
[*]From *Songs for the Pre-School Age,* Broadman Press. Used by permission.

of the Bible verse: "All things were made by him; . . ." (John 1:3).

A song such as "Thank You, God" may be sung at bedtime to help the child express thanks to God for loving care.

Bible stories may be sung to the child such as songs about the Baby Jesus and the Christmas story. As the child grows older, he enjoys other songs about Jesus which tell how He grew and worked and played. Every child who hears "Jesus Loves Me" enjoys it and soon learns to sing it.

Songs that teach Bible truths are important too for the child, such as "Be Ye Kind" or "Love One Another."

Other experiences with music in the home are important to the child too. Sacred recordings may set the mood for the new day. A busy mother may find her soul refreshed and her spirit lifted toward God as she listens to beautiful sacred music while working around the home. Instrumental music played softly in the background during mealtime can deepen the whole spiritual tone of the home. Sacred recordings may be used to bring the family together in the evening in a spirit of worship.

Recordings where Bible verses are used in song and narrative can be played over and over to help children memorize the scriptures. The words thus sing themselves into the hearts and minds in never-to-be-forgotten ways. Poems and songs about the Bible will increase a child's appreciation for the Bible.

Bible verses put to music may be a part of family worship. Some of the grand old hymns of the Church extolling the Bible and the great truths of the Bible may be used also in family worship.

Those of us who have been blessed with a vital Christian heritage remember songs heard in the home that helped to teach us about God and Jesus. My mother loved to sing as she worked. The gospel songs and hymns she sang made deep impressions on me. I well remember one of her favorites:

> *I am so glad that our Father in heav'n*
> *Tells of His love in the Book He has giv'n.*
> *Wonderful things in the Bible I see;*
> *This is the dearest, that Jesus loves me.*
> —P. P. BLISS

Sometimes I did not understand the words in the songs she sang, such as: "Blessed assurance, Jesus is mine . . ."

"What does it mean, 'Blessed assurance'?" I asked.

"It means that we can know for sure in our hearts that we belong to the Lord," Mother told me.

Children are often creative in composing music to sing their favorite Bible verses. If the music can be written down and learned by the whole family, it is a thrilling experience for the child. Sometimes a child's own composition, played when he thinks no one is listening, reveals to us the beauty and depth of his thinking and feelings.

In the Church School

Music is an important part in the church school curriculum. Songs included in the lesson materials are usually carefully chosen and contain desirable concepts and important truths. They are also chosen with the age level of the child in mind and are therefore within the child's understanding.

Experiences with music are most important in the teaching plans of the church school. The experience of singing together unifies the group and brings a togetherness not otherwise obtained. A good song is often an important part of the teaching of a unit. It is a happy way of teaching children what we want them to learn.

A creative group will be able to put Bible verses to

music to be used in the worship time. A beautiful song is also often filled with word pictures which suggest other creative work to the children, such as drawing pictures to illustrate, or writing poems or prayers to express thanks for the truths contained in the song.

The kindergarten child, both at home and in the church school, has many happy experiences with music. He enjoys Bible verses put to music. He enjoys Bible stories found in songs such as "Away in a Manger" and "Baby Jesus Went to Sleep." He enjoys songs about the adult Jesus, such as "Jesus Went About Doing Good." He also enjoys songs about the Bible, as "The Bible Is the Book We Love."

When a child comes to primary years, music is used increasingly to teach about God and the Bible. Such a song as "The Bible Is a Treasure Book" may be used to great advantage in teaching a Bible appreciation unit.

Let us look at the first stanza:

> *The Bible is a treasure book*
> *Of stories that are true;*
> *It tells of people long ago—*
> *Of folks like me and you.* *

This stanza may lead to helpful conversation about stories "that are true" and a recall of important Bible stories. It may help the children to recall ways in which people long ago loved God and tried to serve Him as we do today. It may open up the way for a study of the Bible stories, a search for pictures, and suggest creative activities such as illustrating the stories.

The second stanza also opens to us interesting ways of teaching the Bible:

*From "The Bible Is a Treasure Book," by Elizabeth McE. Shields. Copyright, 1944, by Elizabeth McE. Shields. Used by permission of John Knox Press.

The Bible is a treasure Book
Of verses old and new.
Some make us think of lovely things;
Some show us what to do.

This stanza suggests a search for "verses old and new" to give meaning to the second line. Verses that make us think of lovely things may also be found and discussed. Verses that "tell us what to do" may be recalled and will help the children to understand some of the things we should do. This verse also opens up opportunity for creative drawing to illustrate.

A unit of study on "God Made Our World" may take for its theme a song such as:

God, who made the world of beauty—(Genesis 1:1)
  Sea and skies above—(Psalm 95:5)
Every gift which Thou hast given (James 1:17)
  Tells us of Thy love. *

Such a song helps to summarize learnings about God, the Creator. It may lead to conversation about God, and a search for Bible verses to suit the words. It suggests creative activities, and also may lead directly to worship.

A primary leader was using the song "Tell Me the Stories of Jesus," with a class of third graders. First she discussed the meaning of the various lines of the song.

"What would you ask Jesus to tell you 'if He were here'?" she asked.

Jack raised his hand first. "I would ask Him to tell me a story," he said.

Jerry was next. "I would ask Him to tell me about His power to heal." (Jerry had defective vision. It was

---

*From "God, Who Made the World of Beauty," by Dorothy S. Warren. Copyright, The Pilgrim Press, in *Children's Religion.* Used by permission.

difficult for him to keep up with the other children, but he had real spiritual insight.)

There were several other suggestions, and then Monty raised his hand. "I would ask Him to help me be a Christian," he said earnestly.

There was a moment of silence, and then the group sang worshipfully together:

> *"Tell me the stories of Jesus*
> *I love to hear,*
> *Things I would ask Him to tell me*
> *If He were here."*
> —W. H. PARKER

Information about Bible times is contained in good primary, middler, and junior songs.

Songs also help children to understand what is expected of them in the light of Bible teaching. "Boys and Girls Can Be like Jesus" and "When I Think of Jesus" help primary boys and girls to try to be like Jesus in everything they do.

Middler and junior boys and girls may be thrilled and inspired with some of the great hymns of the Church. A hymn may lead to interesting activities, such as a search for knowledge as to how and when the hymn was written, and what Bible passages and truths are brought to mind by its words. Good gospel songs help in a most effective way to teach God's plan of salvation. Songs about Jesus inspire and lead juniors to commit their lives to Him.

Middlers and juniors enjoy singing some of the beautiful Bible passages put to music such as:

Enter into his gates with thanksgiving.

At Christmas time they enjoy:

Glory to God, glory to God,

Glory to God in the highest;
And on earth peace,
Good will toward men.

Sharing the Bible Through Worship

As we think of sharing the Bible through worship, we may first of all ask ourselves, What do we mean?

Worship in simple terms is feeling *near* to God and feeling God *near* to us. Worship is fellowship with God—fellowship that is very real and precious.

"God is a Spirit:" said Jesus, "and they that worship him must worship him in spirit and in truth" (John 4:24).

Worship then is of the spirit. It is based on what we feel within—a sense of wonder and awe in the presence of God, a spirit of love, joy, thankfulness, and praise.

What better way to develop awe and wonder than through the Word of God itself? What better language for expressing our joy, thankfulness, and praise than through the beautiful poetic passages of the Bible?

Our spirits mount with the Psalmist as we read:

For the Lord is a great God, . . .
O come, let us worship and bow down:
let us kneel before the Lord our maker.
—Psalm 95:3, 6

Our consideration here is how to relate those Bible passages and truths to the child's own experience so that he may truly worship also.

Atmosphere

Children are sensitive to atmosphere. Particularly is it true in worship. It sets the mood and creates the spirit of worship.

The room where the children meet should be as neat and attractive as possible. An open Bible, good pictures, seasonal materials from the out-of-doors, materials pertaining to the unit of study, attractive posters and song charts all add atmosphere conducive to worship.

The teacher or leader is also a vital part of the child's atmosphere. Children are quick to sense our own attitudes, our personal relationship to God, and our capacity for worship. When we come on Sunday morning, with a sense of wonder and awe in the presence of God, we help to create an atmosphere of worship for the children.

Children should be helped to realize that worship is not something static—it is radiant, alive, full of joy. Peter said, it is "joy unspeakable and full of glory."

Thus should all our worship be—joy that enters our singing, the reading from the Bible, our conversation together; joy that finds expression through our voices, our faces, and our testimonies; joy that the children can see, feel, and share.

Meditation

We need to increase our own sense of wonder and awe as we read God's Word if we are to lead children in worship. We need to meditate on Bible verses and passages before we share them with the children.

Think for a few moments on the golden text of the Bible—John 3:16:

For God so loved (the wonder of His love)
that he gave (the wonder of His gift)
his only begotten Son (the wonder of the Lord Jesus himself)
that whosoever (the whosoever that takes us in)
believeth in him (the wonder of faith)
should not perish, but have everlasting life (the wonder of eternal life, forever with Him)

Such meditation should fill us with the wonder and awe of the gospel that we want to put into all our teaching about the Bible and God.

Participation

Another important part of worship is participation by the children themselves. From early days through junior years the child must have a part if he is to worship. In order to plan effective worship services, the supervisor or teacher needs to know what is being done in the other classes in the department, and to use in the worship period what the children are learning in class. It is a time when memory verses may be recalled and longer passages from the Bible used in choral readings. Activities the children have carried on to help learn Bible verses or to make Bible truths clear may be shared with the entire group. Class teaching pictures may be used to recall and retell a Bible story. A responsive prayer may be worked out in the smaller group with a Bible verse as the response, and used during the worship period.

The songs that are chosen, whether a Bible verse set to music or a song about the Bible or one that teaches a Bible truth, may enrich the worship.

The Bible itself in a prominent place in the room and turned to for use during the period is an important part of worship.

Conversation with the children may be definitely worshipful.

A group of middlers were enjoying Psalm 100 together. The children sat in a semicircle with Bibles in their laps. Jennifer stood beside a chart ready to write.

"Psalm 100 is such a happy psalm," said the teacher. "We will read it together. When we come to a happy word, let's stop and Jennifer will write that word on the chart."

How interested the children were as they read together

and then stopped while Jennifer recorded: *joyful, gladness, singing, thanksgiving, praise, thankful, bless!*

It was a happy, worshipful time for all, God seemed very near as the Bible was read and enjoyed together.

For Study and Discussion

1. State briefly in your own words your purpose in sharing the Bible with the children you teach.

2. Study the purposes given in your lesson materials for a given unit. Be prepared to discuss at least two of these purposes with the class.

3. Give an example of when you have led your children in a creative activity.

4. Be prepared to tell a Bible story as you would tell it to a group of children in the age-group you teach.

5. Tell how you would go about helping a group of primary children dramatize a story.

6. List several songs or hymns that have contributed to your own spiritual growth.

For Further Study

Books on Methods

Take It from Here, 1 and 2, Yoder
Teach 'Em like God Made 'Em, Crabtree
Clues to Creativity, 1, 2, 3
New Dimensions in Teaching Children, Robert Fillbright (BR)
The Ministry of Music with Children, by Ethel Bailey (NZ)
Guiding Children, by Elsie Rives and Margaret Sharp

Audiovisual

Consult your publishing house for recommended audiovisual materials.

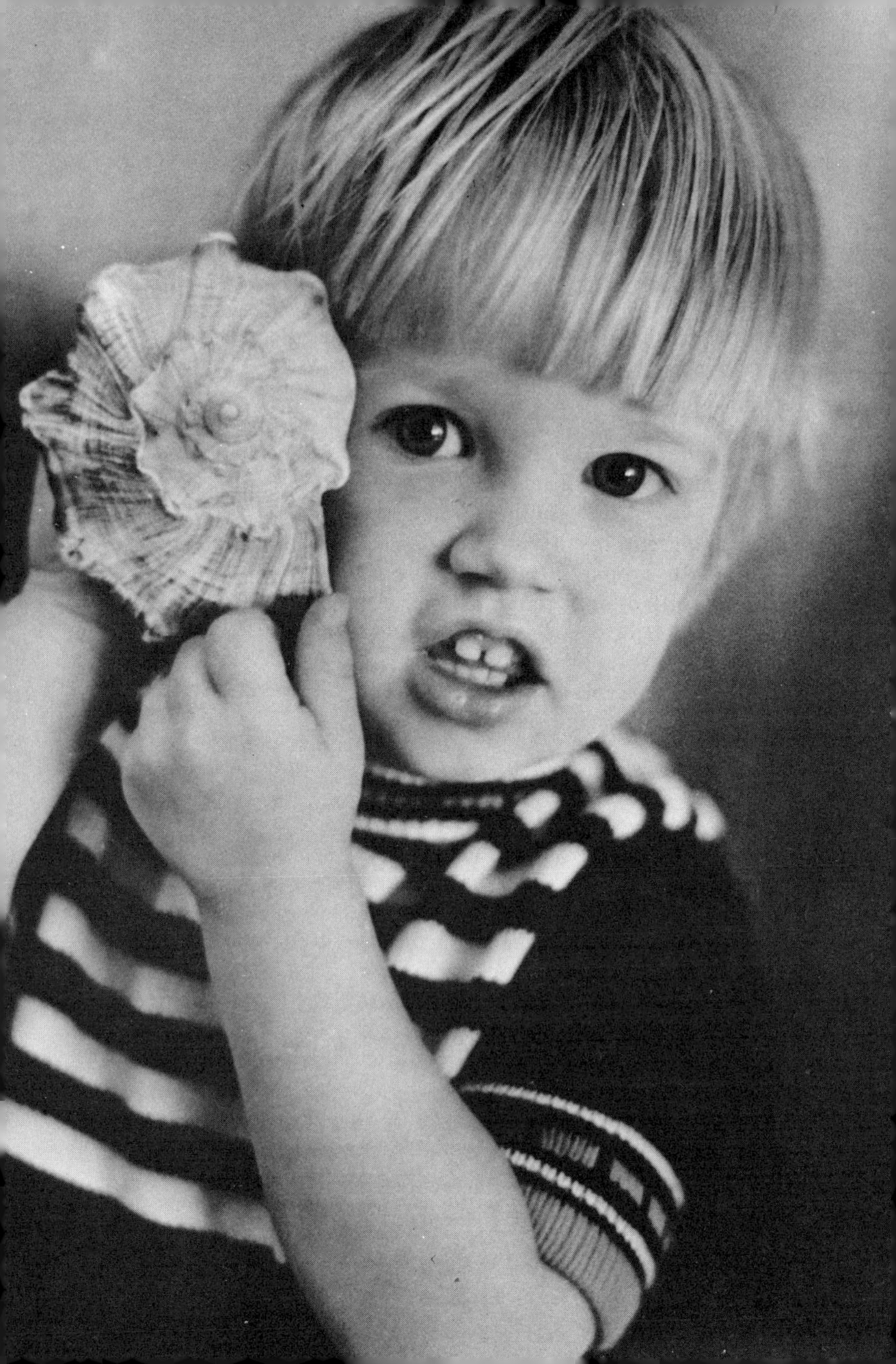

3/

Nothing is so infectious as example.
—CHARLES KINGSLEY

The Bible and the Nursery Child

When do we begin to teach the Bible in the home? Do we start when the child is two years old, or wait until he is three or more? And how do we begin—by telling Bible stories the child can understand?

Indirect Teaching of the Bible

Teaching the Bible to children begins long before we may say, "This is the Bible," or, "The Bible says." We begin with ourselves, what we are and what we strive to be in the light of Bible teaching. Young children are very sensitive to atmosphere; thus our own attitudes toward the Bible is most important. Our love for the Bible as shown through our voices when we speak of it, and our hands as we handle it, says something to our children. The Bible is something very special, we say indirectly over and over again.

We are teaching the Bible too when we exemplify its teachings day by day in the home. Love for one another, kindness, helpfulness, honesty, truthfulness—all speak to our child long before he is old enough to associate these qualities with Bible teaching. "Fruit of the Spirit," we read in Galatians 5:22-23, "is love, joy, peace longsuffering, gentleness, goodness, faith, meekness, temperance . . ." The Christian parent is teaching his child as he manifests these characteristics of the fruit of the Spirit.

The parent who loves the Bible and who is familiar with its beauty and richness may relate the child's experiences to the Bible before he is old enough to understand the Bible verses as such.

A beautiful flower, a budding tree, a butterfly may be just the thing to spark the child's interest and give opportunity for the mother to say: "'God . . . made every thing beautiful,' the Bible tells us."

A child may be enjoying a favorite food. "God gives us our food, the Bible tells us," we say. "Thank You, God, for our food."

This early approach to the use and teaching of the Bible is of greatest importance if our child is to grow up to love and reverence God's Word for himself.

There may be also a more direct approach when the child is quite young. A mother may hold her child in her arms as she reads the Bible. "This is the Bible," she says. "It tells about Baby Jesus."

As the child grows older, he sees Mother and Daddy read the Bible at mealtime or at family worship. He sees the older children in the family read from the Bible or quote verses from memory. He is beginning to understand that the Bible is important to his family.

The Two-Year-Old

Two-year-old Melinda soon learned to associate the Bible with family worship time. When the family came together for worship, it was Melinda who ran to bring the Bible for Daddy or Mother to read. This made family worship a happy time for her because she had a part in it. There were reverence and a quiet atmosphere as a few short passages were read.

Stevie sat on a high stool watching his mother stir up a batch of cookies. Round and round when the big spoon as she mixed in the flour, sugar, raisins, and other ingredients.

"God gives us our food," said Stevie's mother. "He sends the sun and rain to make things grow. The Bible tells us so."

"I like God," said Stevie.

Such conversations may take place often as a mother is preparing food for the family. There is warm, sweet fellowship between mother and child, and the child learns in a wonderful way about God and the Bible.

Interesting and helpful experiences may be enjoyed by the child and mother in planting seeds or working with flowers either in the house or in the garden. It is an exciting experience for the child to behold the miracle of seeds bursting forth into new life and growing in the sun and rain.

One summer when the weather had been unusually hot and dry, two-year-old David and I were out in the yard looking at our wilted flowers. The robins were hiding under the spirea bushes with their wings hanging down.

A sudden clap of thunder sent us scurrying into the house ahead of a wonderful, refreshing shower. Together we stood at the window and watched the rain come down. Now the robins came out of their hiding and hopped about the lawn in sheer delight. The flowers seemed to lift their heads immediately.

"Look at the rain," I said. "The birds and flowers are getting a nice, cool drink."

"Rain, rain!" David laughed and clapped his hands in excitement.

"God sends the rain," I told him. "The Bible tells us so."

It is a thrilling experience for a mother and child alike when the life cycle of a butterfly or moth is observed. From an interesting caterpillar to a sleeping chrysalis, and then a beautiful butterfly—what a wonder it holds! The Bible verse, "The works of the Lord are great," takes on real meaning following such an experience.

The very young child is always fascinated by the stars and moon at night. "God made the moon and stars," we say; "the Bible tells us so."

The Three-Year-Old

In all our teaching of the Bible, whether direct or indirect, we need to keep in mind the needs and limitations of the three-year-old.

1. *The three-year-old learns through sensory experience.*

The three-year-old cannot read, so he depends upon the things he hears, sees, feels, and tastes. Words are not enough; pictures and books are not enough. He must have actual experiences which cause him to wonder and to learn about the goodness of God.

What an adventure a walk around the block may be! A smooth stone to hold in his hand, a robin hopping on the lawn, some busy ants scurrying along the sidewalk are all to be enjoyed and wondered about.

"God made everything," we say. "He made the robins and the ants. We read about it in the Bible."

2. *The three-year-old is curious.*

The walk around the block also arouses the child's curiosity, and his learnings may be related to thoughts about God and the Bible. There are so many interesting things to see and hear. There are so many things to discover and explore.

"Where do the robins get robin food? Why do the ants

run away?" he asks in his eager quest for learning.

"God cares for the robins," we tell him. "He cares for the little creatures like ants. The Bible tells us so."

3. *The three-year-old learns through association.*

Three-year-old Cindy and her mother were watching a beautiful sunset. The sun, a great red ball, was just slipping beyond the horizon. "It looks like a lollipop," cried Cindy. A lollipop was something familiar. It was natural for her to associate the sunset with something she could understand and that had meaning for her.

The three-year-old can respond only to what he knows. His vocabulary is very limited and he thinks only in terms of what he may relate to himself. When we talk to our three-year-old about food and warm clothing, about loving parents, pets, and happy homes, he understands. When we relate these things to God's loving care for us, we foster a growing love and appreciation for God. And when we relate them to the Bible, likewise, we foster a growing love and appreciation for the Bible as God's Book.

4. *The three-year-old needs security.*

Nothing is so important to the child's welfare and spiritual growth as daily care and love in the home. The mother and father who are loving and tender, who take time to have fun and fellowship with the child, are building a firm foundation for the child's faith and trust in God. This does not mean that there will not be a firm, steady discipline, but it does mean that love must shine through every act and experience.

Bedtime with the comforts of warmth, rest, and good-night kiss speaks to the child of the goodness and love of God.

"'God is good,'" we may say. "He gives us our homes and our nice, warm beds." Sometimes we sing softly,

"Thank You, thank You, God."

The child goes to sleep, secure in the love of his home and parents, and with the words of the Bible, "God is good," taking on new meaning. And before the Bible can take on meaning for our children there must be experience and understanding.

5. *The three-year-old is active.*

Both in the home and in the nursery class, an important part of a child's learning is play. It is the world in which he lives. He must have space to play in, and be able to choose his own activities. He must have opportunity to take turns and share. It is through this sharing and playing with others that the child learns to live the truths of the Bible—kindness, helpfulness, friendliness, love—all may become a part of his learning about the Bible.

Materials to Help Us Teach

Few of the larger Bible story books published are suitable for the three-year-old. However, Bible story books designed for the three-year-old in the church school are most valuable for use in the home. The pictures are simple and attractive. The stories are written for the nursery age child and based on experiences which are familiar to him. (See book list at end of this chapter.)

Records for the young child are a wonderful source of enjoyment and of great value in teaching songs about the Bible and simple Bible verses.

Melinda, who at two brought the Bible to the family group at worship time, has a broader concept of the Bible at three. She thinks of it now as a Book that has good stories. It tells about the Baby Jesus.

How Melinda loves the story of Baby Jesus! She lives it over and over again during the Christmas season. She listens while Daddy reads the story from the Bible by candlelight. She knows the song:

Baby Jesus went to sleep
  On a bed of hay;
In a manger soft and deep
  Baby Jesus lay.

Mother Mary tucked Him in,
  Warmed His tiny feet;
Sang a lullaby to Him,
  "Sleep, my Baby, sleep."*

In her play, Melinda becomes Mother Mary, tucking her baby doll in a blanket, warming its tiny feet, and singing to it.

Melinda enjoys other stories from the Bible, too, provided they are not too long—stories about Jesus, a kind Person who helped people. She likes sound effects and short, simple words in the stories. She likes to hear the same story over and over again.

Music helps Melinda to know about the Bible too. She loves to listen to records with songs about Bible truths—sharing toys and playthings. She sings "Jesus Loves Me" along with the artist on the record. She associates simple verses, such as "Be kind," "Love one another," with the Bible.

In the Nursery Class

The child who from the beginning has had happy and satisfying experiences with the Bible in the home is ready for the nurture and training which the Sunday school offers.

As the home first of all teaches what the parents are, so the nursery class teacher teaches first of all what the teacher is. Long before the child can understand Bible stories and truths, he begins to understand these truths

---

*From "Baby Jesus," by Kathryn B. Peck. Copyright, 1940, by Nazarene Publishing House. All rights reserved.

as they are worked out in the lives of the adults around him. The teacher's attitude and manner say something important to the child as she welcomes him on Sunday. She has a friendly smile. She is helpful and kind. She is gentle but firm. She knows how to make the child feel at home.

Happy experiences in the nursery class say something important to the child too. Songs, pictures, books, and activities contribute to his happiness and spiritual growth. The Bible is displayed in a prominent place. It is often referred to and used by the teacher. There are pictures and short stories from the Bible. There are songs about the Bible and Bible truths.

Bible materials for the nursery class are carefully planned with the child's needs in mind. His short attention span is considered and thus stories are brief. The words used are within his understanding. Simple Bible verses are given to be used over and over again.

The sessions in the nursery class are planned to provide materials and experiences within the understanding of the child. The child learns about God, who loves and cares for him. He hears stories about Jesus, the Friend who loved children and helped everyone. He grows in understanding of the Bible as God's special Book. While the Bible stories are short and simple, they have real meaning for the young child. He has happy experiences which foster a growing love for the church. He begins to be aware of others and their rights. He begins to want to be a helper and enjoys simple experiences of working with adults in the church. He is guided to a sense of security and trust in God.

The three-year-old loves repetition. Thus he enjoys hearing the same Bible stories over and over again. He enjoys singing familiar songs or hearing favorite records many times.

Pictures for use in the nursery class are carefully chosen. They must be large enough to attract and hold attention. They should be simple with very little detail. The colors should be soft and appealing. The objects and activities pictured should be those that are familiar to the child.

Bible pictures illustrating stories and Bible truths within the nursery child's understanding may be used effectively. Pictures of Jesus should be simple, clear, and attractive. There should be a permanent picture of Jesus hung at the child's eye level.

Pictures of the out-of-doors that teach love and appreciation for God, the Creator, may be used effectively. Pictures that show Bible truths, sharing, helping, showing love are also helpful in teaching the Bible to the nursery child.

On Sunday Morning

It will be interesting to see how the Bible is taught to a group of three-year-olds on Sunday morning.

Tommy, a three-year-old, is greeted by his teacher with a friendly smile that says, *Welcome, Tommy.* The room says welcome, too. The unit of study is "I Live in God's Wonderful Word," and centers around the creation story. Its purpose is to help Tommy think of God as the Maker of everything good and beautiful. There are beautiful things in the room—early spring flowers and budding branches for Tommy to help arrange.

Activity centers have been attractively planned. Here is a table with interesting things from God's creative work for Tommy to explore and enjoy: a bird's nest, a beautiful shell, some spring flowers. There are pictures too of flowers, leaves, sky, and birds for him to enjoy.

The book center has attractive books open ready for Tommy to see. The children's own storybooks, part of the lesson materials, are here for Tommy to enjoy.

A teacher is ready at the block or doll center to direct Tommy's attention to activities that are related to the lesson purpose.

It is a beautiful spring morning, so a short walk has been planned for the children. The teacher will share Tommy's delight in the blue sky overhead, the new leaves on the trees and shrubs, and the song of a robin in a tree nearby.

"God made our beautiful world," the teacher will say to Tommy. "The Bible tells us so."

Back in the room after the walk, the children will sing "The Wonder Song."

Then with the Bible in hand the teacher will tell the Bible story "God Made Everything."

"A long time ago there were no beautiful flowers, no trees, no grass, no food growing. There was no rain to fall on the land.

"God made many lovely flowers." *(Shows a flower.)*

"God made the tall trees grow to give us shade." *(Shows a leaf or a picture of tree.)*

"God made rain.

"God made the pretty green grass to grow.

"'God . . . made every thing beautiful.'"

Opening the Bible to Ecclesiastes 3:10-11, the teacher will read, "He [God] hath made every thing beautiful."

After the story there will be a song: "Thank You, God, for Flowers" (rain, grass, and other things the children mention).

The teacher will pray briefly thanking God for all these things.

After prayer there will be a special activity in which the children are guided in making pictures that show some of the wonderful things spoken of in the Bible. As the children work, the teacher will repeat the verse, "God . . .

made every thing beautiful."

In many churches today the extended session offers an additional hour for music, rest, Bible story, and conversation with the children. All these add to the use of the Bible with nursery children.

When it is time to go, Tommy is waiting for his parents to come for him. He has had a happy time in Sunday school. He has grown in his appreciation of the Bible as the Book that tells about God's wonderful world.

The work of the nursery class does not end with the morning session, however. At home Tommy relates to his parents the good time he has had. He shows the picture he has made. He sings some of the songs he has learned. Daddy or Mother takes time to enjoy with Tommy his book of Bible stories provided for use in the home.

The church and home are working together to teach Tommy about God and His wonderful Book, the Bible.

For Study and Discussion

1. When do parents begin teaching the Bible to their children?

2. Tell an incident when you have used an indirect approach for teaching the Bible.

3. What is the most important factor in the spiritual growth of the nursery child?

4. In what ways may the church and home work together for the spiritual nurture of the child?

For Further Study

Books for Parents and Teachers

Living and Learning with Nursery Children, Joy Latham
You Can Teach 2s and 3s, Mary A. Barbour
Filmstrip *How Young Is Our Welcome?* Beacon Hill

Books for Twos and Threes

My Bible Book, Janie Walker
My Jesus Book, Frances Hook
My Book of Bible Stories, Frances Hook

Plastic Book Series
- *Baby Jesus*
- *Little Boy Jesus*
- *Thank You*

Tiny Doing Books
- *We Like to Help*
- *We Can Be Kind*
- *We Learn to Share*
- *We Want to Obey*
   Ruth McNaughton Hinds

4/

The Bible and the Kindergarten Child

Four-year-old David was going for a ride in the country with his parents.

"Look out the window, David," said his mother. "You may see something you have never seen before!"

"Will I see a purple dinosaur?" David asked quickly.

David's mother was not surprised at his question. In fact she was not surprised at any question David asked. He was one continual question mark from the time he opened his eyes in the morning until he closed them at night.

Where is God? Why can't I see Him? Does He see me? Why do baby birds fall out of the nest and get killed? Where do they go when they die? How come the leaves fall down? How big do I look to a germ?

David wants to know the *why* of everything. His mother wisely knows that his future development and spiritual well-being depend largely on how his needs are met now. For that reason she tries to answer his many questions sincerely and intelligently. If she does not know the answer, she says so. If she knows how to find an answer, she and David go on the happy quest together. She is careful not to teach him anything now that he will have to unlearn later in life.

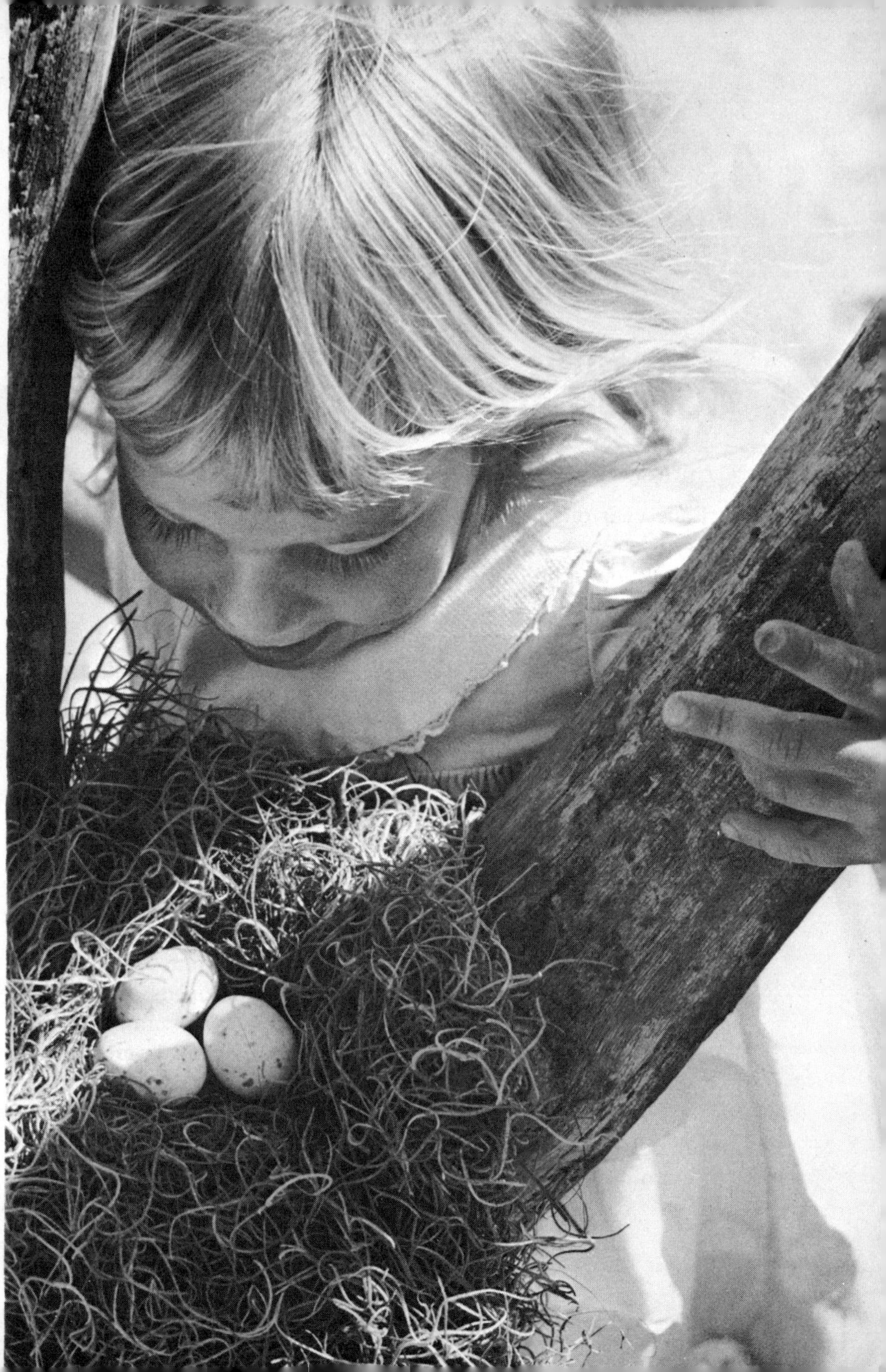

The Four- and Five-Year-Old

Thus David introduces us to the four- and five-year-olds. The child of this age group has many of the characteristics of the nursery child. He is curious. He is still dependent upon his sensory experiences for learning. He wants to touch, taste, feel, and hear. He learns through association with the adults around him and the things which he can experience for himself. He is active and still lives in a world of play. He needs love and security day by day.

In addition to these characteristics we discover some interesting facts about the four- and five-year-olds.

1. *He is developing mentally and spiritually.*

What a world of wonder
To discover and explore,
And oh, so many questions,
When one is only four!

There is rapid mental and spiritual growth in the life of the four- and five-year-old. He is eager to know what is going on around him. His questions about God tell us that he is seeking to find the meaning of life.

Much of the child's real understanding of God as Creator will come through interesting discoveries in the world about him. It is his eagerness to know and his sense of wonder that open up our greatest opportunity for teaching the Bible. He is ready now for some of the beautiful passages of the Bible that will lift his wonder to worship. Thus in the home and in the Sunday school we are prepared to use verses from the Psalms, Epistles, and other parts of the Bible for devotional material.

The child's joy and wonder over the changing seasons may be expressed in verses and selections from the Bible. In the springtime he sees the first little crocus peeping up through the brown earth. He hears the happy song of the meadow lark. The new grass is springing up on the lawn after a warm, spring shower. Now he is ready to understand and enjoy these verses from the Bible:

> *For, lo, the winter is past, . . .*
> *The flowers appear on the earth;*
> *the time of the singing of birds is come, . . .*
> *. . . as the tender grass springing out of the*
> *earth by clear shining after rain.*
> *He* [God] *hath made every thing beautiful . . ."*
> (Song of Solomon 2:11-12; 2 Samuel 23:4;
> Ecclesiastes 3:11)

Or perhaps it is late autumn. The leaves or tumbling down to make a warm blanket for the flowers. The birds have gone away for the winter. The squirrels are hurrying to fill their storehouse before the snow. These verses take on meaning for the child:

> *. . . O give thanks unto the Lord; for he is good:*
> *. . .* (Psalm 106:1).
> *. . . thou hast made summer and winter* (Psalm 74:17).

Sometimes we use a poem to spark the child's interest and then give a verse from the Bible:

> *I like the gentle rains that fall*
> *To help the thirsty flowers,*
> *And give a nice cool drink to all—*
> *And puddles after showers!*

The Bible tells us, God "giveth rain upon the earth . . ." (Job 5:10).

Much of a child's understanding of God who loves him comes through loving care he experiences in the home. When he is secure and happy in the family, he can readily respond to God's love. The opposite is true of the child who comes from a home lacking in love and security. Such a child often has great difficulty relating to the truth of God's love. But children from any home need to discover what the Bible says about God's love and care. They need to know too what the Bible says about loving one another.

"The Bible says . . . 'let us love one another'" (1 John 4:7).

The child's understanding of what God wants us to be and what He expects of us comes through contacts with adults who love God and try to please Him.

> *I like God's loving plan for me*
> *In home and loved ones too;*
> *And I will try in every way*
> *To be more helpful day by day*
> *In everything I do.*

The Bible says, ". . . be ye kind" (Ephesians 4:32), we teach our child.

2. *He is developing skill in creative ability.*

The kindergarten child often imitates the group, but he is also showing more individuality in his activities.

A group of kindergarten children were drawing pictures of flowers to tell of God's springtime gifts. Some of the children were drawing flowers and birds. Stan divided his sheet of paper with a line down the middle. On one side were flowers of many colors with a blue sky overhead and a round sun. On the other side the sky had been darkened with a black crayon and there were marks to indicate raindrops. "It rained," Stan said simply.

There are many creative activities which may be used with the four- and five-year-olds in the home and Sunday school to teach Bible verses, stories, and truths. The child's ability to work with other children encourages group projects such as making a mural to illustrate a

Bible verse. The mural is made from a strip of brown paper or shelf paper, and cut to the size desired. There should be one central theme, and pictures to illustrate the theme may be drawn by the children or cut from magazines and catalogues and pasted on. Picture strips or friezes are also interesting and helpful group activities. (A frieze is a series of pictures illustrating a story, Bible passage, or an idea.) The four- and five-year-olds also like to make scrapbooks or booklets illustrating Bible verses.

Painting is a good medium of self-expression for either individual or group projects. (Be sure to provide aprons for this!)

The child likes to make something at Sunday school to take home, so little seasonal devices such as fruits at Thanksgiving time, cut from construction paper, containing printed Bible verses may be used effectively.

Peep boxes which depict a scene from a Bible story are a never-ending source of delight to the young child.

Working with clay is interesting and helpful, particularly to the timid child or the child who feels repressed.

The very young child may create something very beautiful with words when the sympathetic adult is ready to write down what the child says. The child may put a Bible story into his own words. He may help to form a responsive prayer using simple Bible verses as the response.

3. *He is imaginative.*

Gary was going outdoors to play. His mother saw him open the door and then step aside and wait.

"I'll let Jimmy go first," he said. Jimmy was his imaginary playmate. He and Gary had many happy times together. They talked things over. There was giving and sharing.

Thus we see the four- and five-year-olds enjoy dramatic play. It is a most effective way of making a Bible story live for the child. "Let's play like" is an expression often heard in the home to retell a Bible story or to illustrate a Bible truth. It is used effectively in the Sunday school and may develop during an informal period with the children helping to plan, or following the telling of a story. Simple pieces of cloth may, to the imaginative child, become a whole costume to make the experience more real and enjoyable. The child also enjoys posing pictures especially at Christmas time.

The fours and fives enjoy portraying the emotions of characters in a story. This helps them to enter into the feelings of others.

4. *He learns through conversation.*

Parents and teachers find conversation is a fruitful and enjoyable way of teaching the four- and five-year-old. Sometimes it may lead to a solution of the child's problems and inner needs. It will reveal also a child's wrong concept of a word or phrase, and this gives opportunity for further clarification or corrections by the parent or teacher.

Conversation is important in planning and carrying out activities. It builds warm and loving fellowships between the adult and the child.

Conversation may be directed to learning about God and the Bible. "What does the Bible say?" we wonder, and with the child turn to the Bible to find out.

Conversation may also lead to prayer and worship, both at home and in the church school.

The Four- and Five-Year-Old and the Book

The four- and five-year-old is growing in his concept and knowledge of the Bible as a Book. He understands that it is a special Book which tells about God and Jesus, and tells us what is right and wrong.

A great many more Bible stories may be read and enjoyed with the kindergarten child than with the three-year-old.

The child, through the use of stories and pictures, is forming a clear idea of Jesus as a kind and loving Friend. He is growing in love and appreciation of Jesus, which is laying a foundation for later understanding of Jesus as Lord and Saviour.

We use the story of Jesus' birth, and other incidents of His life within the understanding of the young child. Stories of Jesus which can be related to the child's own experiences are most suitable. These include stories of Jesus out of doors, and His words about flowers and birds, sun and rain. We will also include stories of Jesus helping people, and stories of Jesus teaching us to be kind and helpful.

Old Testament stories about homes, loving care, helpfulness, and sharing are used effectively.

Bible stories for the four- and five-year-old should be 350 to 500 words in length. They should have one central theme, with little descriptive material. Direct discourse is most effective. Sound effects and repetition make stories more interesting to the young child.

Bible story books are enjoyed by the kindergarten child. However, these should be carefully selected. The language should be within the child's understanding and the illustrations clear and in good color without too much detail. Parents and teachers also need to be reminded that not all Bible stories are suitable for the young child. We avoid any stories which may give a child a wrong concept of God. We also avoid stories for the fours and fives that deal too much with violence.

The four- and five-year-old is ready to participate in

the use of the Bible in the home. He may help to dramatize a story for family worship. He may learn such short passages as: "God is good"; "God . . . loved us, and sent his Son [Jesus]"; "O give thanks unto the Lord." He may choose songs about the Bible to sing. He may select a suitable record and operate the record player.

The Four- and Five-Year-Old and His Curriculum

The curriculum materials for kindergarten children in the church school consider the needs and abilities of the four- and five-year-old, and are planned accordingly. Those who develop the curriculum and lesson materials keep in mind the short attention span of the young child and his capabilities. Materials are developed to teach the Bible and Bible truths in the ways best suited to the child in this age-group. While there are special units of study on the Bible itself, there are plans for the use and teaching of the Bible in every lesson. Each lesson contains a Bible story or a story with a Bible background. A "Bible verse to remember" is also included in each lesson. These are carefully selected verses for the children to use over and over again. (See Appendix.) There are selections from the Bible to help the children express joy, praise, love, and thanks to God.

Kindergarten children need many experiences with the Bible if they are to grow in knowledge and appreciation of it as God's Book. They need help in associating stories with the Bible. Therefore the Bible needs to be used and enjoyed each session at Sunday school. There should be a large, attractive Bible in the department or class. It should have a place on a low table where the children may have access to it. Stories of the Bible may be illustrated by pictures cut from their booklets. These may be cut out and pasted on plain paper and then inserted in the Bible where the stories are found. The children will look forward to opening the Bible to these pictures. Only a few pictures should be used at a time, and these should be changed from time to time.

Children also need to learn to associate with the Bible the verses they have learned. They need to be guided into discovering that the Bible contains beautiful songs that help them tell their love and thanks to God. Kindergarten children enjoy the beauty and rhythm of such songs as "I Was Glad" (Psalm 122:1) and "Song of

Joy"* (Psalm 4:7). The teacher should call attention to the fact that these songs are in the Bible. The Bible may be opened up and the verses read to the children.

While there is constant use of the Bible in every session of the kindergarten class or department, we may notice how particular emphasis is given during a Bible appreciation unit.

The kindergarten room itself speaks to the children about the Bible. The large Bible is ready for use by the teacher and children. There are pictures of Bible stories placed around the room. On the Bible table is a large picture of a teacher using a Bible with children. Activities for the morning may include playing a familiar Bible story or scene. There are mounted pictures of Bible stories ready for the children to use and enjoy freely. Handwork activities, such as something to color or cut out to take home, are related to the Bible.

When the whole group comes together for worship, there are happy songs to sing. Bible verses set to music are used and the teacher calls attention to the fact that these songs are in the Bible. A Bible verse to remember is used over and over again in various ways. Attention is always called to the fact that this verse is from the Bible.

A Bible finger play is used in which the children are reminded of some of the things the Bible tells us. The children may open their hands to pretend they are reading Bible verses along with the teacher.

When Bible story time comes, the teacher, with an open Bible in her lap, tells a brief story. It is one that may be related to the child's own experiences, such as a story about helping, sharing, or homelife.

There is further conversation and a song about the Bible. Prayer will include thanks to God for the Bible.

*See *Children's Praises* for these songs.

The Bible and Special Days

The Bible may be made meaningful to children when we use it at special times in the home and church school.

At Thanksgiving time, even a very young child may express gratitude and praise by saying, "God is good." The kindergarten child may have a part in a special Thanksgiving grace at the table by repeating, "We give thanks to Thee, O God."

Christmas is a wonderful time for enjoying the beauty and wonder of the Bible in the home. The children may help to arrange a manger scene on a table or windowsill. The figures should be simple and those which the children may handle many times and enjoy. Carols which tell the Christmas story may be sung over and over. Recordings of Christmas music give meaning to the holiday season.

On Sunday Morning

Let's see how the Bible takes on new meaning and appreciation for Janie during the Christmas season at Sunday school. Janie can hardly wait until Sunday morning comes. So many wonderful things are happening at Sunday school. Little brass bells on the door of the kindergarten room ring when she opens it. And when she steps inside, how beautiful the room looks! There pasted on a window is a candle that Janie helped to make last Sunday. On a low table is a Christmas creche for the children to enjoy. Above the creche on the wall hangs a beautiful picture of the Baby Jesus with His mother, Mary.

Near the work center is a partly trimmed tree. Last Sunday Janie helped to make paper rings to hang on the tree. There will be more to make today. When the tree is finished, it will be taken to a shut-in.

In one corner of the room is a box filled with hay and

a doll wrapped in swaddling clothes. The children had watched the teacher wrap the doll in long strips of cloth as she had said, "This is how Mother Mary wrapped her Baby."

The teacher smiles warmly at Janie and takes her wraps. Then Janie goes to the work center to help make decorations for the tree. While Janie is working, a teacher is there to talk to the children about Christmas. "'God . . . loved us, and sent his Son' (Jesus)," the teacher says. "That is why we do loving things for others at Christmas time."

Later Janie goes to the reading table and enjoys books and pictures about Baby Jesus. A helper is there to direct Janie. While she is looking at the books and pictures, she hears music. The record player is going. Someone is singing, "God loved us and sent His Son. Jesus is His lovely name."

Soon the children are called together. In the group there is conversation about Christmas. There are songs about Baby Jesus. With the Bible in her hand, the teacher repeats the Bible verse, "God . . . loved us, and sent his Son" (Jesus). Then still holding the Bible, she tells the Bible story.

After the story, the teacher sings softly "Away in a Manger."

"Would you like to tiptoe very softly over to the manger?" the teacher asks.

Very, very softly Janie and the other children tiptoe over to the box with the baby lying on the hay. As they stand around the manger, Janie smells the sweet fragrance of the hay. She reaches out and touches a few strands with her finger tips. She joins in singing with the others, very softly, "Away in a manger, no crib for a bed."

After the song, the teacher prays:

"Thank You, God, for sending us little Baby Jesus."

Why was this Sunday morning such a happy, satisfying experience for Janie? She was learning in unforgettable ways the beauty of the Bible. First, there was *readiness.* Janie was eager from past experiences to learn something new today. Second, there was *atmosphere.* The little bells on the door, the appearance of the room, the materials, music, pictures, books, decorations—the teacher herself, everything said welcome to Janie. Third, there were *materials* and *meaningful activities.* Fourth, there was a *Bible story well told,* and a verse to remember. Fifth, the children played the story, tiptoeing to the manger. Sixth, there were Janie's sensory experiences around the manger. Janie was learning in the ways that little children learn.

For Study and Discussion

1. Why should a mother take time to answer a four- or five-year-old's questions?

2. Tell of an incident when you have been able to relate a child's wonder to a Bible verse or truth.

3. Relate a Christmas experience at Sunday school that you recall from your own childhood. If it was a happy one, tell why.

For Further Study

For the Teacher

You Make the Difference for 4s and 5s, by Mary LeBar
You and Preschoolers, by Elsiebeth McDaniel with Lawrence Richards

Books for the Child

My Book of Friends, by Frances Hook
My Thank-you Book, by Frances Hook
My Bible Book, by Janie Walker
Bible Story Book, God Keeps His Promise, by Cornelia Lehn

5/

Primaries and the Bible

When we think of primary children, we think of those who are six and seven years of age. And we ask ourselves as parents and teachers, What are their abilities and their limitations in learning from the Bible? What do they think? How do they act? What can they learn?

We realize that a child's limitations and abilities depend much upon his environment. What he thinks, feels, and how he acts may result from experiences with people, objects, and surroundings. When the parents, teacher, and pastor are aware of these important factors and work together, far more significant work can be done in building Christian character. The parent and teacher who take time to study the general and individual needs of primary children will be far better equipped to meet such needs and to teach the Bible effectively.

The Six-Year-Old

At six we realize perhaps that John is not nearly so well behaved as he was at five. "Are we going backward?" we sometimes wonder in dismay. We realize that John requires more patience and love. He seems to yearn for approval and praise. Then we remind ourselves that at six John has begun a whole area of new experiences, perhaps walking to and from school alone or riding the school bus on his own. He is finding his place in a new and vastly

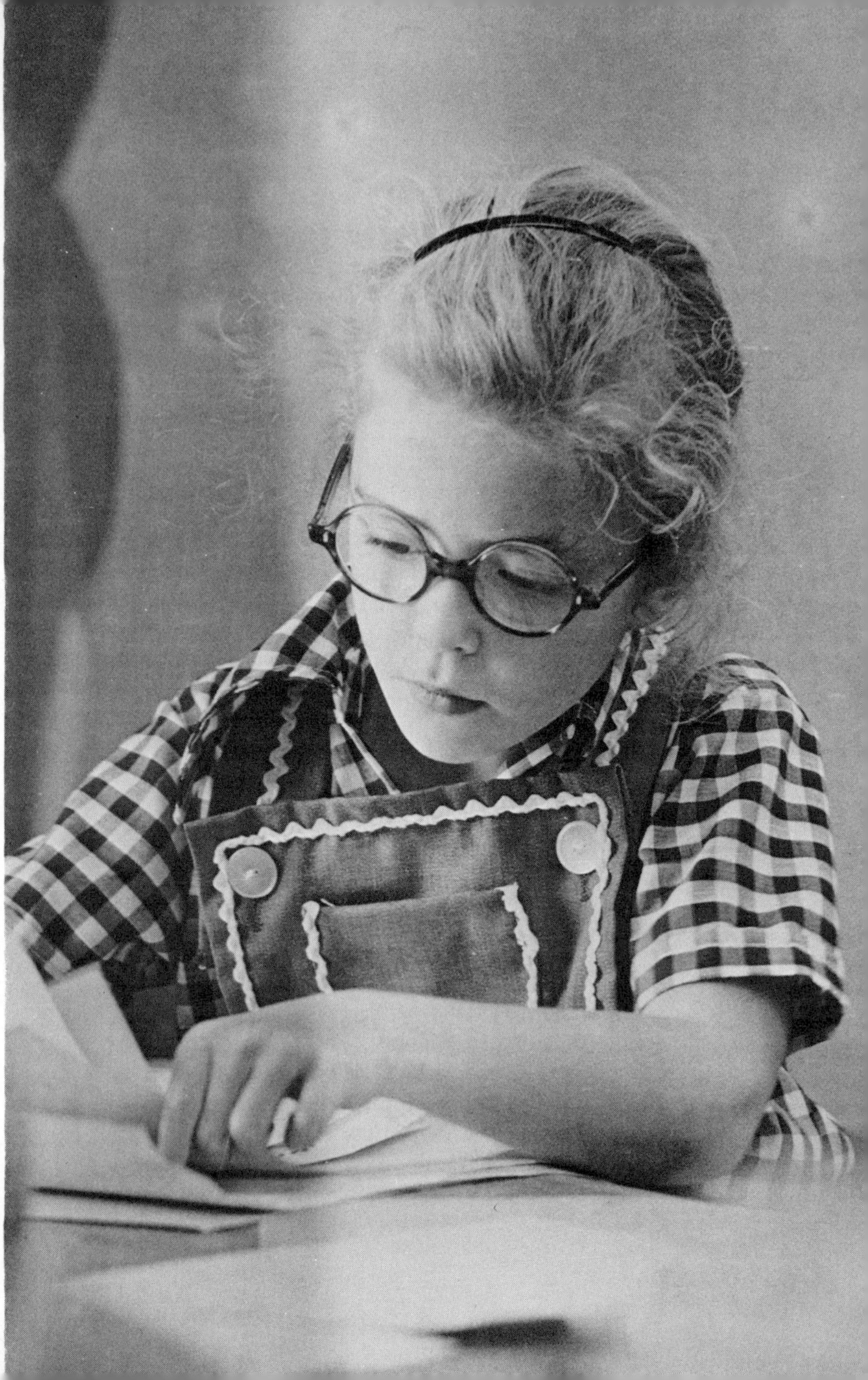

different world. His body is growing rapidly and he is often tired to the point of exhaustion.

When we think of John, we realize that he is growing in spiritual insight too. He wants to know more about God and prayer. He is interested in the Bible and with our help tries to find certain verses, although he cannot read them without help. John is becoming increasingly aware of right and wrong within him. He wants to be good but often is unable to cope with himself. No wonder he is sometimes unstable, explosive, and a problem to parent and teacher alike!

The Seven-Year-Old

By the time John is seven, he is better adjusted and better behaved. "What a good boy John is!" we often say to ourselves and to others. However, he is apt to be too introspective and somewhat of a daydreamer. He is forgetful and loses his belongings. His explosiveness of six has been replaced somewhat with complaining or whining. He longs for approval of his parents and teachers, and other children in the home and school. John is developing a more thoughtful interest in God and asks many questions about God and the Bible.

Thus when we think of the primary child in the home and in the church school, we must think of these different needs and abilities. But in spite of these differences, there are common qualities of the six- and seven-year-old which make our task of teaching about God and the Bible easier.

The primary child's love of beauty, his interest in the world about him, his eagerness to know *why* and *how,* his responsiveness, all open up great opportunities for spiritual growth and development. At home there are more opportunities for family projects and outings than with the preschool child. There may be exciting walks through the woods, trips to the country, vacations, family gatherings, fellowship, and other opportunities for happy, rewarding times together. Good books, good music, fellowship, and fun are invaluable in creating wholesome atmosphere for the growing child.

Teaching the Bible Through People

When we think of people who are important to the child's growth and development, of course we think of parents, grandparents, other relatives, and teachers. Grandparents who live in the home can be a great blessing and living examples of Bible truths. Happy hours spent with a good grandfather who knows how to make and do so many interesting things can help to inspire and mold Christian character in the very young. A wise, devout grandmother, like Grandmother Lois of Bible times, can contribute greatly to a child's spiritual growth and knowledge of the Bible. When a young mother is burdened with many things to do and little time to do them, the grandmother often helps by reading to the child or helping the child to read to her. Good times may be had together reading the Bible and Bible story books, or stories that teach Bible truths. Grandmother may also help a child commit passages to memory or teach songs with Bible verses. She may also teach a child the importance of prayer, and the privilege of telling our needs and problems to a kind and loving Heavenly Father. Often it is Grandmother who teaches a child to memorize the Lord's Prayer.

The Bible in Primary Curriculum

Well-planned primary curriculum materials are Bible-centered, and are planned to give the child as much of the Bible as is within his understanding. They are planned to give a clear picture of God and the Lord Jesus.

We want always to tell Bible stories and teach Bible

truths which give the children a picture of God as revealed in Jesus Christ, and a deeper appreciation of Jesus as the Son of God.

Primary children are ready to know something of the plan and theme of the Bible. They are interested in learning that it is in two parts, the Old and New Testaments, and are interested in learning what each part contains. They like to discover where to find the story of Baby Moses, Baby Jesus, and others.

With primary children, the most valuable stories, of course, are those which are simple and deal with familiar experiences, child life, homes, and worship. Pictures and storybooks are valuable in helping primary children to know and understand the Bible.

Stories of Bible people who knew and loved God are important. Those who were true to God through adversity and persecution help children develop courage and steadfastness in their own lives. Learning about Bible people whose lives were changed by the Saviour helps them to know they too can find forgiveness and eternal life through Him.

Bible material is also included to enrich the children's own worship and provide words that will help them tell their love and praise to God.

When we choose Bible material for the primary child we need to think of his abilities in connection with the Bible. He can read simple verses; he is interested in Bible background material, how people lived and what they did. He enjoys learning new things, and is imaginative. He can create beautiful song poems, and draw pictures which illustrate his feelings.

The primary child is still in a world of play and therefore dramatic play is valuable as a teaching procedure. The primary child loves to go on a quest for learning and is able to help evaluate the work of the group.

Primary Children Enjoy Activities

A group of primary children were studying a unit entitled "Our Daily Bread." The children decided to make a frieze for their bulletin board. First a large strip of wrapping paper was cut to the size of the bulletin board. Then it was divided into three portions, a group of children being responsible for each division. The first group decided to make a seed chart. Their heading was "We Thank God for Seeds." They brought seeds from home and mounted on the chart with gummed tape. Then a picture was drawn of the plant, vine, or tree from which the seed came. The finished chart contained drawings of plum and peach trees, cantaloupe, pumpkin vines, and wheat, all with the seeds neatly taped nearby. A Bible verse, "O give thanks unto the Lord; . . . Who giveth food to all. . . ." (Psalm 136:1, 25), was printed at the bottom of the chart.

The second group decided to illustrate selections from Psalm 74.

. . . God is my King of old, . . .
The day is thine, the night also is thine:
. . . thou hast made summer and winter.
(Psalm 74:12, 16a, 17b)

The children made drawings of a summer harvest scene with a bright sun shining, and a nighttime winter scene with moon and stars. The drawings were first sketched in with chalk and then colored with crayon.

The third group of children entitled theirs "Helpers Who Work with God." They drew individual pictures of farmers, milkmen, a baker, a farmer's wife gathering eggs, a little girl milking a cow, and other helpers. For the Bible verse to print at the bottom of their finished work they chose "For we are labourers together with God . . ." (1 Corinthians 3:9).

A class of primary children in vacation Bible school had a thrilling experience making a Palestinian house large enough for them to enter. First, there were discussion and planning. There was research and a list was made of materials needed for such a project. The materials were gathered and then the work began. A large packing box became the house. It was covered with brown wrapping paper which extended above to form the parapet. Some of the children wove paper mats for the floor. The ingenious teacher rigged up a bicycle wheel to serve as a potter's wheel. The children (well aproned!) fashioned pottery vessels on the wheel from wet clay. These vessels were allowed to dry and then painted with tempera paints. Other children made a mezuzah (a cylinderlike box containing Bible verses placed on the doorpost of the Jewish home) to put on the doorpost. This was made from a cardboard roller, such as is found in paper towels. The roller was cut in half lengthwise and one-half fastened with gummed tape to a flat piece of cardboard. Inside the mezuzah was placed a small scroll with the Bible verses, Deuteronomy 6:4-5 (the Shema) printed on it. As the children went in and out of the little house, they followed the Jewish custom of putting their fingers to their lips and then touching the mezuzah to show their love for the Word of God.

This project resulted in the children learning much about early Bible times and helped them to feel at home with Bible people. It also helped them to realize the importance of God's Word to people long ago, and they grew in their own appreciation of the Bible.

Other Activities

As with the kindergarten child, peep boxes are a source of enjoyment. These may be made to depict a scene from a Bible story and used to retell the story to others. Table scenes and dioramas are also useful with primary children.

A picture roll makes an interesting project. Pictures may be cut from old leaflets and other sources, or drawn by the children to illustrate stories of the life of Jesus or other Bible narratives. These are pasted on a strip of shelf or wrapping paper which is fastened to rollers. The rollers are placed in a box with a picture window in front, and turned to show the pictures. Children may recall the stories as the pictures are shown.

Similar to this is the *kamishibai*. This is a box with an opening in front to show the pictures. Flat pictures are inserted through a slit in the top of the box to illustrate Bible stories or truths. The children may choose pictures, mount them on cardboard, and manipulate them as they tell Bible stories to the group.

Rebus charts are enjoyed by the children. The charts, recalling Bible stories or short stories about Bible people, may be printed in newsprint, wrapping paper, or shelf paper, omitting the nouns. The children may draw pictures or cut out pictures to paste in the blank spaces.

Interesting ways may also be devised by the creative teacher to teach Bible memory verses. The verses may be printed on heavy cardboard and cut into puzzle shapes for the children to arrange. The verses may be printed also on flannel-backed paper and cut into separate words. The children enjoy arranging words on a flannelboard to complete the verse or arrange it in proper order.

Flash cards are effective too. Pictures illustrating a Bible verse may be on one side and the Bible verse on the other. Or lead questions may be printed on one side and answered by a Bible verse printed on the other side.

Primary children enjoy quizzes about the Bible. "Oh, no," they may say, "not a test!" But then they will enter into it and thoroughly enjoy it.

Riddles about Bible people are interesting and helpful. For example:

I was a shepherd farmer.
God told me to go to a new land.
I took my family, my sheep and cattle and went to
   a new country.
There I built an altar and worshipped God.
Do you know my name?

A triptych to use on the Bible table is interesting for the children to make and offers opportunity to use and illustrate Bible verses. This is a three-paneled screen made from cardboard and the panels hinged together with tape. Sometimes the middle panel is made higher than the side panels. The center panel may provide a background for a picture of Jesus or a Bible scene. Bible verses may be printed on each of the side panels.

Accordion booklets may be made with original drawings by the children to illustrate the teachings of the Bible such as showing love, kindness, and helpfulness. The books may be made by fastening four or more sheets of cardboard together with tape. The children's drawings may be made on white paper and then pasted on the cardboard.

On Sunday Morning

Let's visit a primary group on Sunday morning and see how the Bible is being shared.

This is the last session of a Bible appreciation unit, "The Bible, God's Wonderful Book."

The children at the Creative Activities Center have made a shepherd scene. The tent is made from an old sheet, colored with crayons by the children. The scene depicts Abraham and his family enjoying Bible stories of long ago. The figures were provided by activity sheets in the curriculum material.

The children at the Worship Center have made booklets entitled "Songs from the Bible." Covers were made from black construction paper cut to look like a Bible. Inside were verses, mainly from the Psalms. The children had drawn pictures to illustrate the verses.

The children at the Art Center have made a wall frieze entitled "Stories from the Bible." A strip of shelf paper has been divided into four parts. Pictures have been drawn to illustrate scenes from one of the Bible stories.

The children at the Reading Center plan to dramatize a story of the lost scroll for the entire group this morning. They have made simple head scarves from old muslin, colored with crayon. The scroll was made of brown paper and spools for the knobs.

At the Music Center a song chart, "The Bible Is a Treasure Book," is on an easel. Other song charts about the Bible are ready too.

The record player is ready with recordings of songs and verses from the Bible. It will be used during the worship period today.

The Reading Center has a Bible story book and books about the Bible for research. Cassettes, Show'N Tell, and View-Masters all with Bible stories for listening and viewing are available. (These are especially valuable for new children and those with little knowledge of the Bible.)

At the Game Center games have been selected which will help the children recall Bible facts and memory verses. Puzzles and quizzes are also available for children to use in recalling the unit.

At the worship time there will be a recall of Bible memory verses through flash cards. Large teaching pictures will be used to recall Bible stories. Some of the things made by the children at the learning centers will be shared with the large groups. It will be a happy, rewarding time for the entire group.

We will visit another primary group during the Thanksgiving season. How beautiful the room is! How much the whole atmosphere seems to say, "Come, let us worship."

The bulletin board has pictures of the Thanksgiving season attractively arranged by the children. In the center is a large cornucopia with colored fruits cut from construction paper spilling out in abundance. Beneath are the words: "Unto thee O Lord, do we give thanks."

On the wonder table are many interesting things to see: a cocoon, a gall, some acorns, and a picture of a saucy squirrel. There is an interesting bouquet of seed pods and a picture of a child at prayer. On the table is a card with the printed words, "The earth is full of thy riches."

The reading table has several colorful books with seasonal pictures. Illustrated poems have been mounted and are there for the children to enjoy.

At the interest table the Bible is open to Psalm 100. On an easel nearby is an illustrated poster of this psalm which the children have made. A song chart which the children have illustrated with cutout pictures, "Gifts from Our Father," is also ready to use.

The children are busy packing a basket with gifts of food for a shut-in. As they work, the record player is playing, "Father, We Thank Thee." This song will be used later in the worship. When the basket has been packed, a streamer which the children have made—a ribbon with letters cut from gold paper, and this verse, "We have thought of thy lovingkindness"—will be placed over the top to add beauty and meaning to the gift.

The children have written a prayer to use in their worship today. A Bible verse is used for the response:

For our homes and those who love us,

Unto Thee, O Lord, do we give thanks;
For food to eat and clothes to wear,
Unto Thee, O Lord, do we give thanks;
For sun and rain and harvesttime,
Unto Thee, O Lord, do we give thanks;
For summer, winter, spring, and fall,
Unto Thee, O Lord, do we give thanks;
For schools, and friends, and churches,
Unto Thee, O Lord, do we give thanks;
For Jesus, our Friend and Saviour,
Unto Thee, O Lord, do we give thanks;
For a chance to love and help each other,
Unto Thee, O Lord, do we give thanks.*

Thus the Bible is being shared today in rich and varied ways

The Child's Own Bible

A child is always thrilled to receive his own Bible. Parents and teachers should choose wisely in selecting a Bible for the child. The type should not be too small and should be easily read. If there are illustrations, examine them carefully. Sometimes otherwise nice editions of the Bible have garish illustrations which give a child distorted impressions. Avoid illustrations showing violence or cruelty, or those making Bible characters unattractive. It is better to give a Bible without illustrations than one with unsuitable pictures.

During primary years, children should be encouraged to start the habit of daily private devotions. When the child receives his own Bible or passes a milestone such as a birthday or New Year's day, the wise parent often suggests the practice of daily Bible reading and reading of

*From *When You Need a Special Story.* Copyright, The Warner Press. Used by permission.

devotional books perhaps at bedtime. In addition to books which give meaning to Bible verses, there are a number of daily devotional booklets prepared for children. (See "For Further Study.") These are most helpful in encouraging a quiet time of devotion each day.

Teaching About Jesus as Saviour

During primary years as the child becomes increasingly aware of two forces battling within him, there is opportunity for teaching about Jesus the Saviour, as revealed in the Bible. In the Christian home it is not unusual for a primary child to make a decision to follow Christ and to accept Him as Saviour.

The older primary child is ready to understand the meaning of such verses as John 3:16:

"For God so loved the world, that he gave his only begotten Son, that whosoever believeth in him should not perish, but have everlasting life."

The child who is aware of wrongdoing when he wants to do right, and who feels the weight of unforgiven sins, will understand and welcome the verse:

"If we confess our sins, he is faithful and just to forgive us our sins, . . ." (1 John 1:9).

How can we lead a primary child to know the joy of salvation? How can this great Bible truth become his own experience? Again, the godly lives of parents, grandparents, teachers, and minister play an important part. There may be conversation with the child explaining Bible terms and truths. We may use spiritual songs and Bible verses at worship time. There may be the reading of Bible stories and stories that teach Bible truths (see "For Further Study"). Last, and very important, is the warm personal testimony of the adult who knows the wonder of God's redeeming grace in his own life. Thus primary children are often led to the reality of a personal experience of salvation.

Mark and his mother always had a happy time reading from a Bible story book at bedtime. But on this particular night after the reading of a story, Mark seemed troubled.

"What is the matter, Mark?" his mother asked.

"I don't even know if I am a Christian," said Mark.

"Would you like to pray and talk to God about it?"

"Yes," said Mark.

Together they knelt to pray. After prayer Mark seemed happy and satisfied but said little.

The next day Mark came down to breakfast with a self-conscious smile on his face and said, "Well, Daddy, this is the first day."

"First day for what, Mark?" asked his father.

"First day for being a Christian," said Mark confidently.

Did Mark fully understand this experience? Probably not, but who of us understands the mystery of what happens when God speaks peace to our hearts and we know that we belong to Him?

Sometimes the unusual happens in the church school too when the wise and perceptive teacher under the leadership of the Holy Spirit senses a child's awareness and need, and is able to lead him to Christ.

Jimmy was such a child from a fine Christian home. During a unit of study on "Jesus Teaches About God," and a session on forgiveness, the discerning teacher discovered that Jimmy felt the need to be forgiven. He wanted to be a Christian, he said. Teacher and child had prayer together and Jimmy was led into the very presence of God.

Following the Sunday school session, he went into the sanctuary to sit with his grandmother during the morning worship service. And Jimmy wanted to tell his grandmother all about his experience at once.

"It is church time now, Jimmy," said his grandmother. "Let's not talk."

"But, Grandmother," said Jimmy, "it's all right! This is about God!"

Indeed it was about God. Jimmy had met Him in a very real and important way. Later he told his whole family about his decision and that now he was a Christian. There was a definite change in Jimmy from that day and a continuing growth in Christian ways.

The child who is six or seven—what a privilege and what a challenge to direct their steps toward God through Bible teaching!

For Study and Discussion

1. Write a sketch about a child you know who is six or seven.

2. Tell of the influence of a godly adult on your spiritual growth as a child.

3. List five questions children might ask about God and Jesus and how you would answer them.

4. What Bible stories are most suitable for use with primary children?

5. Prepare a short rebus, telling a Bible story, leaving blanks for the children to fill in with words or pictures.

6. Describe a method you have used in teaching a Bible memory verse to primary children.

7. Reread carefully the descriptions of the classes visited. Make a list of all the ways the Bible was being shared in each session.

For Further Study

Books for Primary Children

Tell Me About God—Tell Me About Jesus—Tell Me About Prayer, Mary Alice Jones
Egermeier's Bible Story Book (revised)
Great Bible Stories for Children, by Lane Easterly (Regency)
The Story of Jesus, by Elizabeth B. Jones (NZ)

Devotional Books for Children

Because God Made Me, by Elizabeth B. Jones
Jesus Loves Me, This I Know, by Rolf E. Aaseng (Augsburg)
Let's Talk about God, by Margaret J. Anderson (Bethany Fellowship)

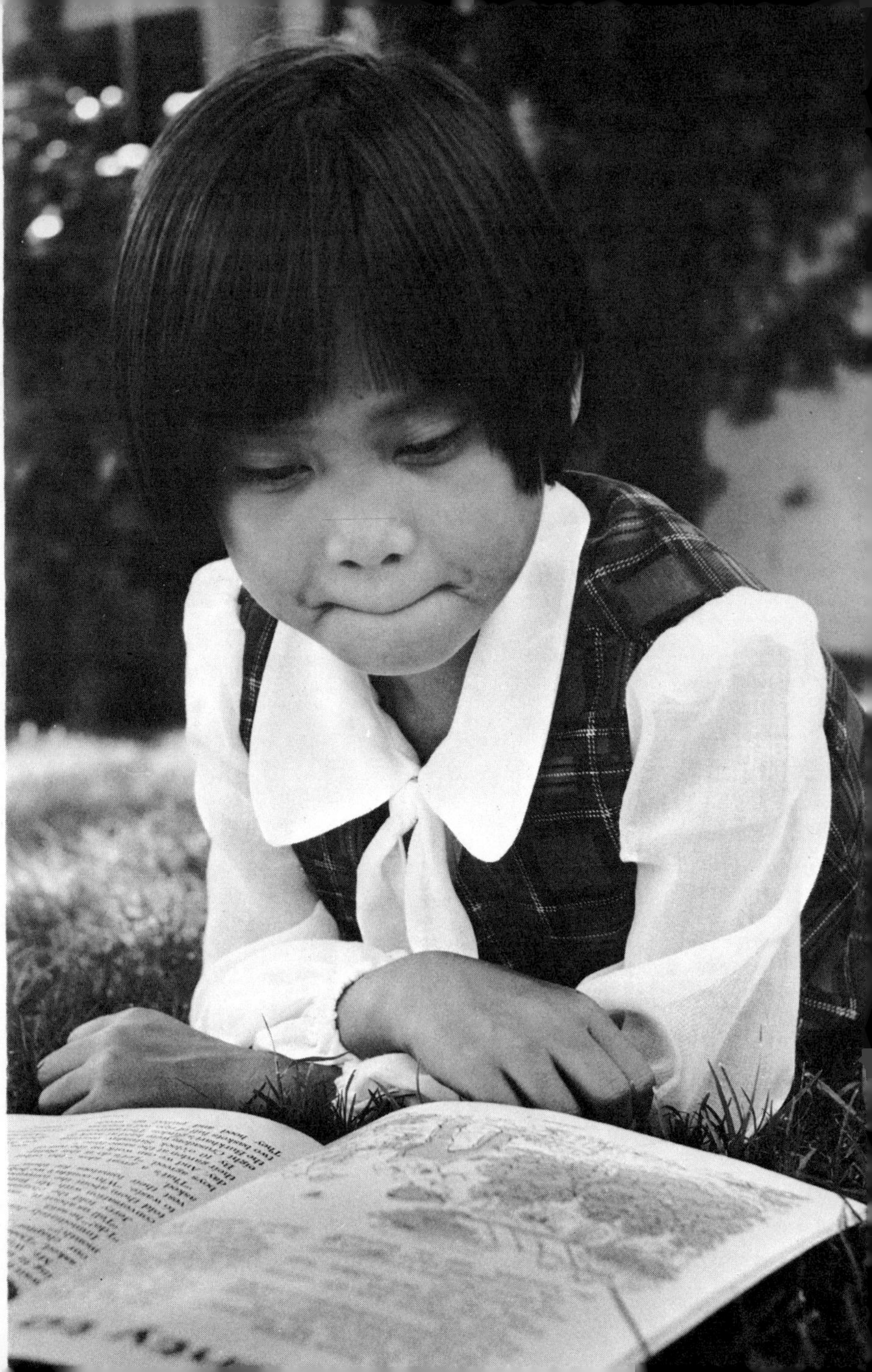

6/

One ship drives east and another drives west,
  While the self-same breezes blow;
It's the set of the sails and not the gales,
  That bids them where to go.

Like the winds of the seas are the ways
  of the fates,
  As we voyage along through life;
It's the set of the soul that decides the goal,
  And not the storms or the strife.*

Older Elementary Children and the Bible

How often parents and teachers of growing children look into their bright, eager faces and wonder what life holds for them! What gales of adversity, disappointments, testings, and hardships lie ahead? We would shield them from these things if we could, but we know that is impossible.

It *is* our responsibility, however, to try to "set the sails" that will largely determine the course they take, and whether or not they will be successful in riding out the storms as they come. Much of the "setting of the sails" depends on us, what we are and what we teach. We do our utmost to give our children a true sense of value and a knowledge of spiritual truth to guide them, but we cannot

---

*Poem, "Wind of Fate," by Ella Wheeler Wilcox. Copyright, the Conkey Company, in *World's Best Loved Poems*. Used by permission.

make their final decisions. We can only do our best, and then watch them embark, with a prayer deep in our hearts that they will ride through the storms and come out safely on the other side.

There is an important element of timing which we must remember and thus take full advantage of the days that are given us to teach our children.

We are told by those who have made the experiment that if a baby squirrel is taken into captivity, when he reaches a certain stage of growth, he will show a great interest in storing away food, as is the nature of all squirrels. But if he is not allowed to do so, the desire seems to pass away forever and he forgets about it. If he is later released in the world to care for himself, he will starve to death. Does this not say something important to use as we think of sharing the Bible with our children?

There is probably no better opportunity to give the Bible meaning and make it a Guidebook for life than during these older elementary years. Thus we need to ask ourselves, How can we best share the Bible with children during these important years?

PART ONE

Let's Look at Middlers

The world is an exciting place for eight- and nine-year-olds. They are in a period of rapid growth and development. Their growing skills and intellectual development are expanding at a rapid rate. They are finding new meaning to life through reading, observing, and listening. The world about them is beginning to come into sharper focus. They can come to logical conclusions that are based on things rather than ideas. The child at this stage is still very literal-number-minded, however, and still has some difficulty with symbolism. He demands realism and thus the most effective method of teaching is through real experiences, objects, games, and activities.

The eight-year-old is in a creative period and responds to activities which enable him to use his creativity. Thus art and dramatic activities are especially effective methods of teaching/learning.

The eight-year-old is learning to relate to the group and enjoys games and other group activities. He is more aggressive about making friends and likes small groups or clubs.

The eight-year-old has courage and likes to make decisions. He enjoys responsibility and likes to work on committees or plan a worship time at home or at Sunday school. He is beginning to understand himself and to accept some of his own limitations and skills.

The child of this age is building his sense of values for a lifetime. He observes evidence of fair play, cooperation, acceptance of others, concern for others, and respect in the grown-ups around him.

The nine-year-old is also developing at a rapid rate. He yearns for independence and the opportunity to decide some things for himself. He is becoming more group-conscious and more able to help carry out activities and projects in the group.

The nine-year-old is more capable of independent reasoning. He likes conversation with his peers and with adults as several ideas are discussed. He enjoys research and looking up answers to questions and problems.

The eights and nines are growing in spiritual insight and an understanding of Bible truths. They are growing in ability to distinguish between right and wrong, and see the importance of making right choices.

Their interest in science and the world about them opens up the door to teaching about the universe and the wonders of God's laws and design. A wonder table with objects from the out-of-doors, books, pictures, and printed Bible verses will arouse interest and help children relate these wonders to God's creative and sustaining power.

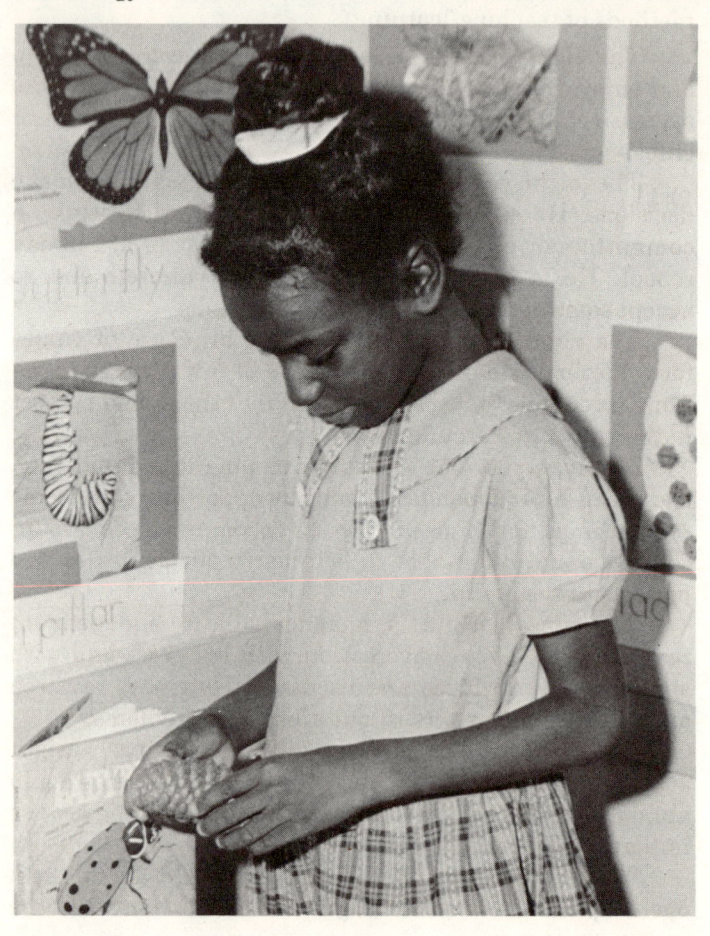

Their growing knowledge of history and the sense of chronology increases their interest in Bible stories and events. Their love of heroes makes the study of Bible heroes effective.

Eights and nines are interested in prayer and are growing in ability to express their needs and feelings to God in prayer. Stories and incidents from the Bible where people prayed and God answered are especially helpful.

Middler children can begin to see more clearly the story the Bible tells, from Genesis to Revelation—the story of God's redeeming love. This helps them to know that God is seeking them today and offering them His salvation through Jesus Christ. God's love as shown through His forgiveness for sin and wrongdoing gives them confidence that this love is for them too. Thus they need not carry the weight of guilt and sorrow when they feel they have done wrong.

The building of a strong self-concept is important to the middler child. Understanding and supportive parents and teachers can do much to help children feel they are important in the home, at Sunday school, and to God. The middler age is an exciting period for teaching the Bible and Bible truths both at home and at Sunday school. Because Bible teaching is neglected or absent entirely in many homes, the church and Sunday school must strengthen its teaching in every way. In these days of bus ministry, many children are brought in on Sunday morning without any previous knowledge of the Bible. Special helps and materials need to be made available to teachers and workers with these children.

Many middler boys and girls have received their first really nice Bible and want to use it when they bring it to Sunday school. But they must have opportunity to use their Bibles, or their enthusiasm will soon wane. The wise teacher plans for at least one opportunity each week for the children to use their Bibles. "Let's find it in our Bibles" adds interest to Bible verses they will use.

Children should be encouraged also to use their Bibles at home in private and family worship times. The children may be asked to report on their reading during the week, and any questions may be discussed. Activities should also be planned to help middlers learn more about the structure and organization of the Bible.

Bible learning at Sunday school should begin as soon as the first child arrives. If there are learning centers, the child should be given opportunity to choose activities according to his interests wherever possible. Bible learning may take place through games, art activities, music, research, reading, and planning for worship time.

The work done at these centers may all be shared in the large-group time.

In the large-group time, there will also be music, conversation, and Bible memory activities. The large-group time will also include the Bible story and prayer.

In the class or small-group time, the pupil book is an important activity. This includes Bible-related puzzles, completion exercises, open-end stories, and activities, all of which help the child relate Bible teaching to life experiences. Games may also be used with these small groups as time allows.

There are no limits to interesting Bible activities for middlers. Creative writing, interviews, TV panels with Bible characters, field trips with cameras, and script writing to go with slide presentations, are all planned by creative teachers and children. Dramatization of Bible truths and concepts all help the children relate the Bible to their own experiences.

Memory Work for Middlers

The Bible verses to memorize for middlers are chosen to help them remember important Bible truths. These key verses should have meaning apart from other verses.

Longer select passages should be chosen for their beauty and meaning to middlers.

All Bible memory verses and longer passages should build up the child's storehouse of verses "for doctrine, for reproof, for correction, for instruction in righteousness" (2 Timothy 3:16). Verses should also be memorized to enrich the child's vocabulary and language for worship. The child's spiritual resources should be built up for life's experiences through "exceeding great and precious promises" (2 Peter 1:4). Verses should be memorized which help a child "grow in grace, and in the knowledge of our Lord and Saviour Jesus Christ" (2 Peter 3:18).

A suggested list of Bible verses and longer passages for middlers is given in the Appendix.

PART TWO

What About Juniors?

All the ways in which children learn are important to remember when we teach the Bible to juniors, those who are 10 and 11 years old. We will need to make use of all our skills and resourcefulness if we are to make our teaching effective, for juniors are *ready to go*. They are active, alert, and thirsty for knowledge. They are doers. If we do not give them something interesting and constructive to do and think about, they will think up things to do on their own. There could be no better motto for juniors than this verse from the Bible: "Be ye doers of the word, and not hearers only."

Juniors are usually strong physically. Just past the most active stage for contagious diseases common to children, and not yet in the critical years of adolescence, juniors are at the peak of physical health. They have abundant energy, partly because of this physical well-being.

Juniors are curious. Their world is rapidly expanding and they are eager to explore. This opens up the way for a quest of knowledge about the Bible. They like to record their own findings in notebooks and on posters or charts.

Juniors have ability to make and carry out their own plans successfully. They have initiative for doing creative work.

Juniors are group-conscious. They like to follow the leader in their own group, and usually present a solid front to the adult leader. They desire approval of other juniors and will often do things to capture attention. Self-conscious, they often giggle or laugh when they do not understand or accept what the teacher is saying.

This group-consciousness can be used to good advantage in teaching juniors. Because they work well in groups, many such projects can be carried out successfully. Committees are effective where juniors work together on special assignments such as map making, dioramas, friezes, and special reports. Shared findings are of real interest to the entire group.

The junior is inclined to be skeptical. He is much concerned with the physical world about him. In the home and in the church school, we need to avail ourselves of every opportunity to teach "Thus saith the Lord."

While all of these traits are common to the 10- and 11-year-old, there are some differences too. As a rule, the 10-year-old has reached a level in his emotional development. Usually, he's cooperative, agreeable, and makes friends readily.

The 10-year-old enjoys family activities and relationships. He very much wants to be a part of the group both at home and at Sunday school. At this age boys want to be with boys and girls with girls.

The 11-year-olds are nearer to puberty and experience emotional and behavioral changes. A child of this age is apt to be clumsy and awkward in his movements. He may be easily upset and often resort to tears. Because of rapid growth in this period the child may appear tired or lazy at times.

Adults, both parents and teachers, need to be understanding and patient during these growing years.

The junior children are growing in spiritual insight also. They are capable of deep feelings and response to God's love. They are giving serious thought to God's plan for their lives and should be encouraged to put God first in all their future plans.

Juniors and the Bible

In teaching the Bible to juniors, there are definite goals we expect to attain.

1. *The junior needs to obtain a good mastery of the Bible as a book.*

The junior lives in a world of books—he is bookconscious, and needs to understand the Bible as the greatest Book of all. He should learn the general structure of the Bible and to feel at home in using it. He will begin to use the Bible as a Textbook for study, research, and reference.

Juniors should learn the books of the Bible in their proper order. This will help them find Bible references readily, and the skill will remain with them through a lifetime of reading the Word.

2. *The junior needs to understand the Bible as the Book of God's message to us.*

The Bible is the Book which reveals God—His ways and His will; and Jesus Christ—His life, teachings, and the salvation He offers.

3. *The junior needs expanded teaching about God as the Creator of all.*

The junior's growing knowledge in the world of science, his eagerness to know the Source of life and power, help us to say, "In the beginning God . . ." The junior needs a growing concept of God, His love, His works, and His will as revealed in the Bible and the world about us.

4. *The junior needs to know more of the power and wisdom of God.*

The junior requires help in relating his growing knowledge to the power and wisdom of God. He needs to understand more and more that "underneath are the everlasting arms." Thus we strengthen our teaching with more about the greatness and majesty of God as revealed in the Bible. Such teaching should enable the junior to realize that God's power is sufficient to help him to be the kind of person he wants and needs to be.

5. *The junior needs a clear picture of the Lord Jesus.*

The junior needs a growing revelation of the Lord Jesus as God's Son, who came into the world to give His life that we might be saved. We expect juniors to understand God's plan of salvation as revealed through the Lord Jesus, and to accept Christ as Saviour.

From a Bible study of the life and teaching of Jesus, juniors should receive a clear picture of the One to whom we ask them to dedicate their lives. Juniors are inclined to hero worship; thus we offer them the Greatest Example the world has ever known. They learn about our Lord's matchless life of love and service for others, His bravery in the face of peril, and His poise and confidence in spite of ridicule and persecution. They discover His gentleness with those who suffered, His eagerness to help, and His sheer abandonment to the complete will of God. As parents and teachers, we ask juniors to accept the Lord Jesus as a Pattern for their lives and to strive to be like Him.

6. *The junior needs to know how our Bible came to us.*

Juniors are developing a historical sense and are ready to understand how our Bible came to us down through the centuries. They can understand the chronological order of the Bible. They can appreciate Bible background material and the geographical and historical background of the people.

7. *The junior needs to regard the Bible as a living Book.*

Juniors must learn to regard the Bible as a Guidebook for their lives. They should establish regular habits of reading it for instruction and help. God's laws are just and right, but they are not always easy. The junior needs to know what is expected of him as a Christian.

8. *The junior needs to know something of what the Bible teaches about the Holy Spirit.*

Juniors are ready to understand the Holy Spirit as God's Helper in the world. The Holy Spirit draws us to God and convicts us of our sins. The Holy Spirit whispers to our spirits and tells us that we are the children of God. He helps us to understand the Bible. The parent or teacher whose own heart glows with the warmth of the Holy Spirit, and who cherishes His presence in his/her own life, is best prepared to teach the junior about the Holy Spirit.

9. *The junior needs to understand some of the symbolism of the Bible.*

Juniors should understand the meaning of the sacrament of the Lord's Supper. They should understand the meaning of baptism. They are ready to understand what Jesus meant when He said, "I will make you fishers of men," and, "I am the good shepherd."

The Junior and His Curriculum

A good junior curriculum takes into consideration these facts and these aims for teaching the Bible. There may be definite Bible units such as: "A Look at My

Bible," "Keeping the Commandments Today," "The Living God," and "The Life of Jesus."

The teacher's guide will suggest a variety of suitable activities such as newsreels, friezes, murals, posters, notebooks, charts, illustrated booklets, and making of puppets of Bible characters. Help will be given for teaching memory work, dramatization of Bible stories, choral readings, and other interesting projects. Suggestions are made for research and Bible study. Space is provided in pupil books for recording findings. Ways are suggested for relating new learning to old. The pupil's workbook will contain quizzes, true and false tests, multiple-choice sentences, blanks to fill in, and other activities for busy juniors.

As with middlers, games are most effective in teaching juniors Bible facts and concepts. Juniors also enjoy field trips, and exploration of God's world. One junior group, while studying a unit on creation, took their cameras to the park and spent Saturday exploring and taking pictures. Later they wrote the script to go with their slides and made a public presentation in the church sanctuary. This activity was most rewarding to the juniors and to all who enjoyed the presentation.

Mapmaking is especially interesting to juniors. Making a map of Palestine will help them to learn many geographic and historical facts about the land where Jesus lived. Outline maps may be purchased from a school supply house and developed by the juniors. Picture maps may be secured from your publishing house with the outline work already done.

Table maps of the life of Jesus or of Old Testament heroes are interesting projects. A foundation map may be enlarged on brown wrapping paper. The junior may draw pictures illustrating Bible stories. These may be colored, cut out, and mounted on cardboard with standers on the back. The children may make palm trees, shepherds, sheep, and wells. The Temple may be placed in the proper location.

Juniors enjoy making spatter-print hanging using Bible verses. This is a good activity for vacation Bible school or an extra class activity on Saturday.

Making a diorama is an excellent way for juniors to learn facts about people of Bible times, and also to help them remember Bible stories. A diorama is a three-dimensional scene in a box. The juniors decide the scene they want to develop and do research to determine the background and what the scene should contain. This requires picture study and search for information in the Bible and books on Bible background. While some of the juniors are working on the background, others may work on figures for the scene.

Bible stories for juniors should be dramatic and vivid. Some of the most effective are those taken directly from the Bible itself, such as the thrilling stories from the Book of Acts. Juniors enjoy stories of Bible heroes. They want to know what these Bible people were like and what they did. They like biographies and therefore enjoy continued stories of Joseph, David, Moses, Abraham, and others.

They enjoy a unit on the Old Testament such as "Adventures with God."

Creative writing is an interesting activity. A report of a Bible incident or event as it may have been written by a present-day news writer brings Bible events to the present-day setting. Juniors can plan a TV interview of a Bible character or a panel of several characters. With a teacher's help, they can plan an entire newspaper of events in Bible times.

Juniors are interested in books with information about the people, customs, and ways of living in Bible lands. They enjoy colored slides, filmstrips, and other visual aids that help them to discover historical and geographical facts about the Bible.

Juniors need books of science to strengthen their study of God, the Creator, and to teach them the dependability of God. They need biographies of missionary heroes and leaders of the Church of the past and present to teach them courage and devotion.

Music

Music is an important part of teaching juniors about the Bible. Bible verses set to music are enjoyed by the boys and girls and are helpful to them in learning these verses. Some of the fine songs about the Bible increase the junior's appreciation for it. These include: "For Stories Fine and True" and "Holy Bible, Book Divine." Songs that teach Bible truths are equally important. These may include "I Would Be True" and "Dare to Be Brave."

Juniors thrill to the beauty of some of the great hymns of the Church. Unfamiliar words and ideas should be explained when the song is first introduced. The new words may be written on the blackboard and discussed with the juniors. Pictures may be chosen to explain ideas and terms. Murals may be painted to illustrate songs.

Thus they will have real meaning and inspiration for the junior.

Pictures

As with other age-groups, pictures are valuable for juniors in their quest for knowledge about the Bible. The use of a picture with a Bible passage or a Bible memory selection gives meaning and understanding. A picture also suggests activities the junior may carry out in the study of the Bible. Present-day pictures help to interpret Bible truths as they show children in real-life situations. Such pictures lead to discussion and a clearer understanding of what the Bible teaches.

Collections

Juniors are collectors. Therefore a collection of interesting objects is helpful in study of the Bible. Objects from Palestine, old and unique Bibles, different translations, and pictures of ancient scrolls are fascinating to juniors.

Bible Memorization

During junior years boys and girls should be guided into memorizing Bible verses and passages which will change their lives and build into the very warp and woof of their characters such qualities as honesty, kindness, truthfulness, thankfulness, and courage. What a child learns as a junior gets into his thinking and helps to form his understanding, outlook, and attitudes for a lifetime to come.

Will a junior forget the actual verses he learns? He may, but the character traits built into his very being will not be lost.

Junior memory work is usually chosen in connected

passages, with additional key verses which tell of God's plan of salvation, and other verses important to the child's Christian growth. Juniors should sometimes be permitted to choose from a selected group the passage they desire to learn.

When we teach memory passages to juniors, we first arouse interest in the meaning of the passage and develop appreciation for the beauty of the expressions. The passage is discussed and unfamiliar words or ideas are explained. Some of the words may be written on the chalkboard. Pictures may be found to help clarify difficult ideas. Maps, charts, and objects may also be helpful in understanding the passage. There may be a discussion of why this particular passage was written.

Learning is a matter of helping the learner to discover the personal meaning of the information for him. Thus the Bible passage we want to teach a junior must be related to him personally. He must discover the meaning of the passage for him and apply it to his own behavior and attitudes. One may help the junior to do this by relating a life-situation story and letting him decide the right thing to do in the light of the Bible passage.

Bible memory passages may take on rich meaning when used by the junior on special days of the year. A psalm given as a choral reading at Thanksgiving time may have rich meaning for junior boys and girls. The Christmas story given as a part of a worship period becomes deeply significant.

There needs to be a frequent recall of memory passages to give added meaning and experience. This may be done through dramatization, the making of illustrated charts or scrapbooks, or the selection of suitable pictures to illustrate. The passages may be used frequently in worship.

When shall we teach these additional memory passages? Time is limited on Sunday morning. Thus the church and home must work closely together if the most effective work is done.

When David was a junior in Sunday school, his church, home, and scouting worked together to help him learn Bible passages and to apply them to his own experience. His Cub Scout motto, "I'm Third," hung on the wall above his bed. ("God First, Others Next, and I'm Third.") He read his Bible daily and frequently asked help in committing longer passages to memory. Later this memory work helped him to achieve his "God and Country" award in scouting. But the most important outcome was the influence the Bible passages had on his attitudes and behavior during his formative years and on to young adulthood.

The Older Elementary Child and Adult Fellowship

The adults the middler and junior know and have fellowship with make a great contribution to his spiritual growth and development. It is through contact with people in the home and in the church who know and love God and who live according to the Bible teachings, that the child receives his clearest picture of Bible teaching.

Children of these years are interested in the worship services of the church congregation. They may join in the joyful singing of the hymns. They may pray when others pray. They like to use their Bibles and follow the reading of the Bible passages. They should be encouraged to listen to the sermon and discuss it later at home. Any difficult words or terms may be explained at these times. The older child senses the presence of the Holy Spirit as the people worship together.

These children should regard the minister as their friend and feel that he is deeply interested in them and their welfare. They become increasingly interested too in the work of the minister and pray for him in family and private devotions.

Prayer meetings whether in the home or at church are important to the developing child. There he comes in close contact with the mature Christians of the congregation. The warm fellowship and glowing testimonies, the Bible verses quoted, the praise and thanks offered for answered prayer, and the sharing of one another's joys and burdens make unforgettable impressions on the young mind.

In the Home

In the home these years are most important for

sharing the Bible too. Family activities during these years are perhaps the most enjoyable of any age. Many happy times may be enjoyed with the family group out of doors and within the walls of the home. The children are now old enough to enjoy family vacations and outings to the utmost. They are not yet old enough to want to go on excursions of their own.

The child's rapidly expanding world, his boundless energy, and his wholesome sense of well-being add up to happy times for all when the parents are understanding and enter into his interests and activities. Love of adventure makes vacation time interesting and instructive. The wise parent takes every opportunity to point the child's eagerness to learn to an appreciation of God, the Maker of heaven and earth, as revealed in the Bible.

A walk in the woods in the fall, the crackle of dry leaves underfoot, the softness of the pine needles, the interesting seed pods, the acorns, the call of the wild birds overhead, the chatter of the squirrels as they hurry to fill a winter storehouse, may print indelibly on young minds the words of the Bible, "The Lord is good to all."

A walk in the springtime when the first wild flowers peep through the brown leaves, the joyous call of the meadowlark, the spring peepers, the opening buds to take home, remind us, "While the earth remaineth, seedtime and harvest, the cold and heat, . . . shall not cease" (Genesis 8:22).

A trip to the lake or seashore, with the many treasures to discover and bring home for collections and study, teach us in a wonderful way, "O Lord, how manifold are thy works!" A trip across the water on a ferry with the huge porpoises rolling and tossing in the water, the water birds darting here and there in search of food—how much fun such a trip can be for all the family! Such outings send the whole family to the encyclopedia or library for new knowledge and information, and add to an ever-increasing appreciation of such verses as, "O Lord, how manifold are thy works! in wisdom hast thou made them all . . ." (Psalm 104:24).

There are times in the lives of each of us that call for courage too. The sudden storm; the unexpected danger; the serious illness, disappointment, or even death of a loved one, call for help beyond our human strength. Children need to know that help comes from such verses as, "The Lord is my light and my salvation; whom shall I fear?" (Psalm 27:1), or, "Yea, though I walk through the valley of the shadow of death, I will fear no evil" (Psalm 23:4), or, "The Lord is full of compassion and mercy" (James 5:11, NASB). In our family we have known all these experiences while our children were growing up. What a blessing it was to present a united front as a family, and to turn to God and the *Bible for help and comfort!*

When tragedy struck a young family recently and two young boys were drowned, the grief-stricken mother said, "I couldn't have made it without prayer and my Bible."

* * *

It is a winter evening. A warm fire crackles in the family room. TV and radio are shut off. Now it is worship time. Father leads in singing "What a Friend We Have in Jesus" or perhaps there is a sacred recording on the stereo. Then the Bible is read and enjoyed together.

"O come, let us worship and bow down: let us kneel before the Lord our maker. For he is our God . . ." (Psalm 95:6-7).

The family prays together, asking God's protecting care through the night, and help for tomorrow.

There must be such times of worship and fellowship in our families if young lives are to be nurtured and trained in the Christian faith; if our homes, churches, and Christian faith are to survive our present age. Let's share the Bible with our children.

For Study and Discussion

1. Read a unit of the lesson materials you are using with middlers or juniors: list *(a)* the Bible passage given for study; *(b)* suggestions for study; *(c)* suggested activities; *(d)* suggestions for teaching memory work. List what is given for pupils to do, such as multiple-choice statements, quizzes, and tests.

2. Reread carefully the session outlined in the chapter. List ways the Bible is being used with middlers or juniors.

3. Choose a Bible teaching activity you have never used before and try it with your class. Report the results.

4. Write in your own words how you would relate a Bible memory verse to a live situation a middler or junior might experience.

For Further Study

For the Teacher

Guiding Children, Elsie Rives and Margaret Sharp
You and Children, Elsiebeth McDaniel and Lawrence Richards
New Dimensions in Teaching Children, Robert G. Fullbright

For the Children

Finding Your Way Through the Bible
Bible Stories: *God at Work with Man,* Mary Alice Jones
Egermeier's Bible Story Book (revised)
Really Living booklet

The Biblearn Series:

Joseph the Forgiver, Jester Summers
Jesus, God's Son, Saviour, Lord, Eugene Chamberlain
Abraham, Man of Faith, Elsie Rives
Paul the Missionary, Iva Tucker
Peter the Prince of Apostles, Muriel E. Blackwell
Moses, God's Helper, William E. Young

BIBLE MEMORIZATION PLAN

Nursery

"God is good."—Psalm 73:1.
"God made everything beautiful."—from Ecclesiastes 3:10-11.
"Love one another."—John 13:34.
"His name was called JESUS."—Luke 2:21.
"Jesus went about doing good."—from Acts 10:38.
"We are helpers."—from 2 Corinthians 1:24.
"Be kind to one another."—from Ephesians 4:32.
"We give thanks to God."—Colossians 1:3.
"God cares for you."—from 1 Peter 5:6-7.
"God sent His Son."—from 1 John 4:10.
"Jesus loved us."—from Revelation 1:5.

Kindergarten

"In the beginning God created the heaven and the earth."—Genesis 1:1.
"Do what is right and good."—Deuteronomy 6:18.†
"What time I am afraid, I will trust in thee."—Psalm 56:3.
"Give thanks unto the Lord; for he is good."—Psalm 118:1.
"I will not forget thy [God's] word."—Psalm 119:16.

"I was glad when they said unto me, Let us go into the house of the Lord."—Psalm 122:1.

"You shall love the Lord your God with all your heart."—Mark 12:30.†

"You shall love your neighbour as yourself."—Mark 12:31.†

"God so loved the world, that he gave his . . . Son."—John 3:16.

"Love one another."—John 13:34.

"Jesus . . . went about doing good."—Acts 10:38.

"We are labourers together with God."—1 Corinthians 3:9.

"Be . . . kind one to another, tenderhearted, forgiving one another."—Ephesians 4:32.

"Children, obey your parents . . . for this is right."—Ephesians 6:1.

"God cares for you."—1 Peter 5:7.†

"God . . . loved us, and sent his Son."—1 John 4:10.

"God is love."—1 John 4:16.

Verses recommended for kindergarten memorization have been quoted from the King James Version of the Bible. Those marked † are also based on this version but have been paraphrased to make them more easily understood by the kindergarten child.

Primary

Genesis 1:1*
Genesis 28:15
Psalm 37:3a
Psalm 56:3*
Psalm 86:5
Psalm 100:1-5
Psalm 118:1a*
Psalm 119:160a
Psalm 121:2

Psalm 122:1*
Psalm 145:18a
Proverbs 20:11
Hosea 14:9
Matthew 1:21bc
Matthew 6:9-13
Matthew 28:19-20
Mark 12:29-31*
Luke 2:11

Luke 2:52
Luke 6:31
Luke 19:10
John 3:16*
John 13:34ab*
John 14:3
John 15:14

Acts 20:35b
2 Corinthians 9:15
Ephesians 4:32*
Ephesians 6:1*
Colossians 3:17a
Hebrews 13:6
1 John 4:10-11*

Extra Credit: Psalms 95:1-7; 117; Luke 2:8-16; John 14:1-6

*Verses marked with an asterisk have been repeated from the kindergarten list. Of the 36 passages recommended, 26 are new to primaries.

Middler

Genesis 1:26a
Exodus 20:3-17 (shortened version)
Psalm 23:16
Psalm 100:1-5*
Psalm 104:24
Psalm 119:11
Matthew 6:9-13*
Matthew 7:7
Matthew 28:19-20*
Mark 12:29-31*
Luke 19:10*
John 1:12
John 3:16-17*
John 10:10b
John 13:34-35*
John 14:3*

Romans 3:23

Romans 5:8
Romans 6:23
Romans 10:13-15
2 Corinthians 5:17
2 Corinthians 9:15*
Ephesians 2:8-9
Ephesians 5:25b-26
Philippians 4:13
Colossians 3:17a*
2 Timothy 3:16-17
1 Peter 1:15-16
1 John 1:9
1 John 3:23
Revelation 3:20

Extra Credit: Psalms 96:1-9a; 113:1-5; 121:1-8; Romans 10:9

*Primary selections to be reviewed. Of the 35 passages suggested, 25 are new to middlers.

Junior

Exodus 20:3-17 (shortened version)*
Psalm 1:1-6
Psalm 23:1-6*
Psalm 103:1-2,
   8-14, 22
Psalm 119:105
Proverbs 3:5-6
Isaiah 53:3-6
Malachi 3:8, 10
Matthew 5:3-12
Matthew 5:16
Matthew 6:9-14*
John 1:12*
John 3:16-17*
John 10:10
Acts 1:8
Acts 1:11
Romans 1:16
Romans 3:23*
Romans 5:8*
Romans 6:23*
Romans 10:13-15*
Romans 12:1
1 Corinthians 6:19-20
2 Corinthians 5:17*
Galatians 5:22-23
Ephesians 2:8-9*
Ephesians 5:25*b*-26*
Philippians 4:13*
1 Thessalonians 4:14, 16-18
2 Timothy 3:16-17*
1 Peter 1:15-16*
1 John 1:7
1 John 1:9*
Revelation 15:3-4
Revelation 21:3-4

Extra Credit: Romans 10:9-10; Ephesians 6:10-17; books of the Old Testament; books of the New Testament

*Repeated from middler list. The junior list contains 35 passages, of which 20 are new to juniors.